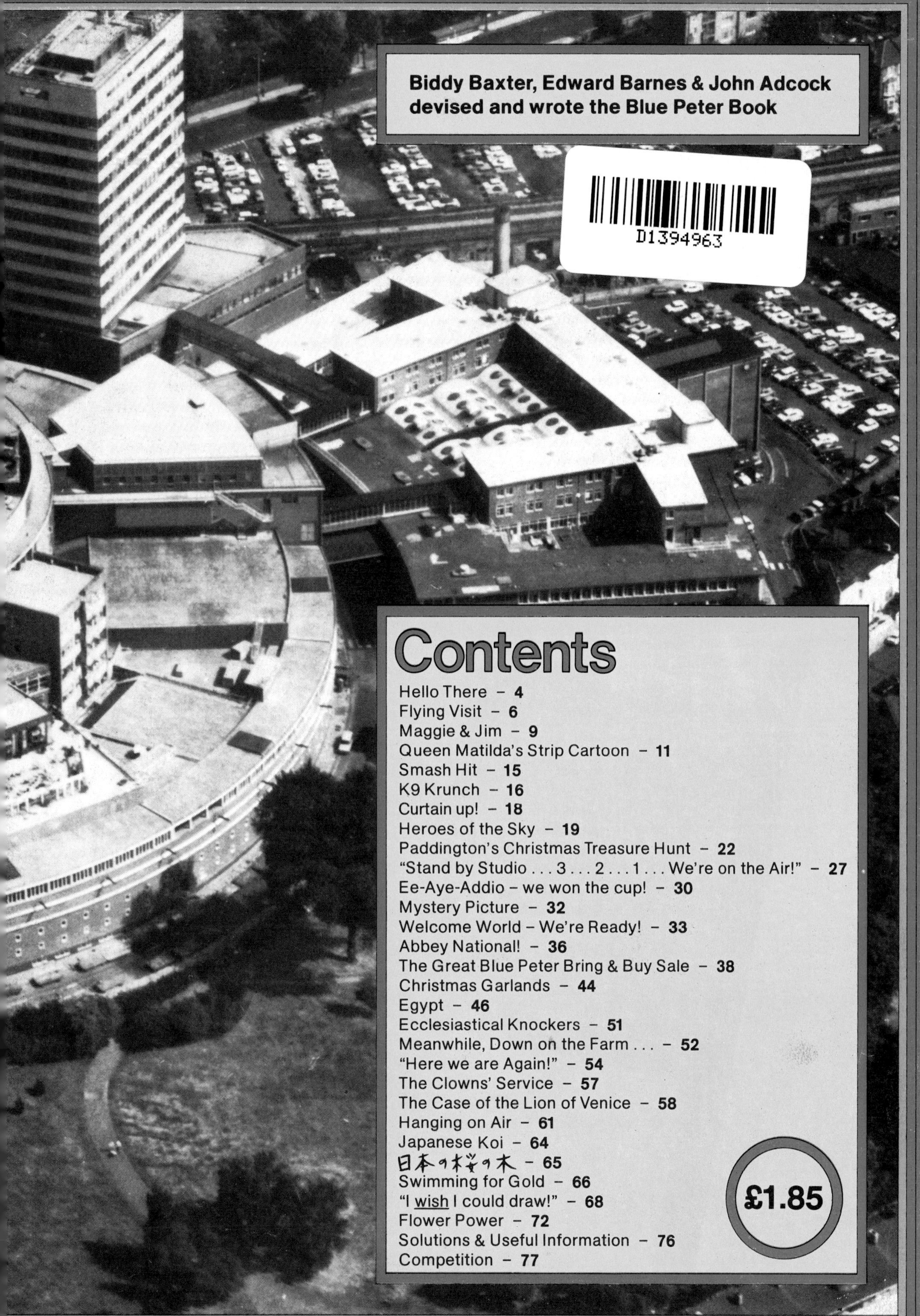

Biddy Baxter, Edward Barnes & John Adcock devised and wrote the Blue Peter Book

D1394963

Contents

£1.85

Hello There!

And with our seventeenth book comes a record of what's probably the most momentous year in Blue Peter's history.

When we launched our Great Blue Peter Bring and Buy Sale Appeal last November 1st, never in our wildest dreams did we expect Blue Peter viewers to provide £3,670,624 worth of aid for the starving babies, children and adults of Cambodia.

We'll never be able to say enough "thank-yous" to all the people who contributed. We just hope that the photographs and the report on pages 38 – 43 will be a lasting record of something that's nothing short of a miracle, for all the readers of this book who helped.

It's been an exciting year and one thing in particular that's cheered us up has been all your letters and good ideas for the programme. It's like Christmas morning every day of the week in the Blue Peter office when Stan, our postman, arrives with his trolley full of letters, cards and parcels!

"What on earth will they think of next?" we say to ourselves as we read how you've dug up a half-a-million-year-old fossil on the beach, or hatched a chicken from an egg from the fridge, or taught a rabbit how to show jump!

It's not a very tidy office – but it's certainly cheerful! The notice boards and walls are plastered with your drawings, paintings, photos and letters. And during our Appeal we even managed to squeeze in a Great Blue Peter Bring and Buy Sale stall amongst all the desks and typewriters.

One very sad thing that happened during the year was the death of Honey, Blue Peter's first-ever Guide Dog for the Blind. Honey was provided from the proceeds of our 1964 Appeal and after she'd passed all her tests, she became the "eyes" for retired school teacher, Miss Elsie Whitehead.

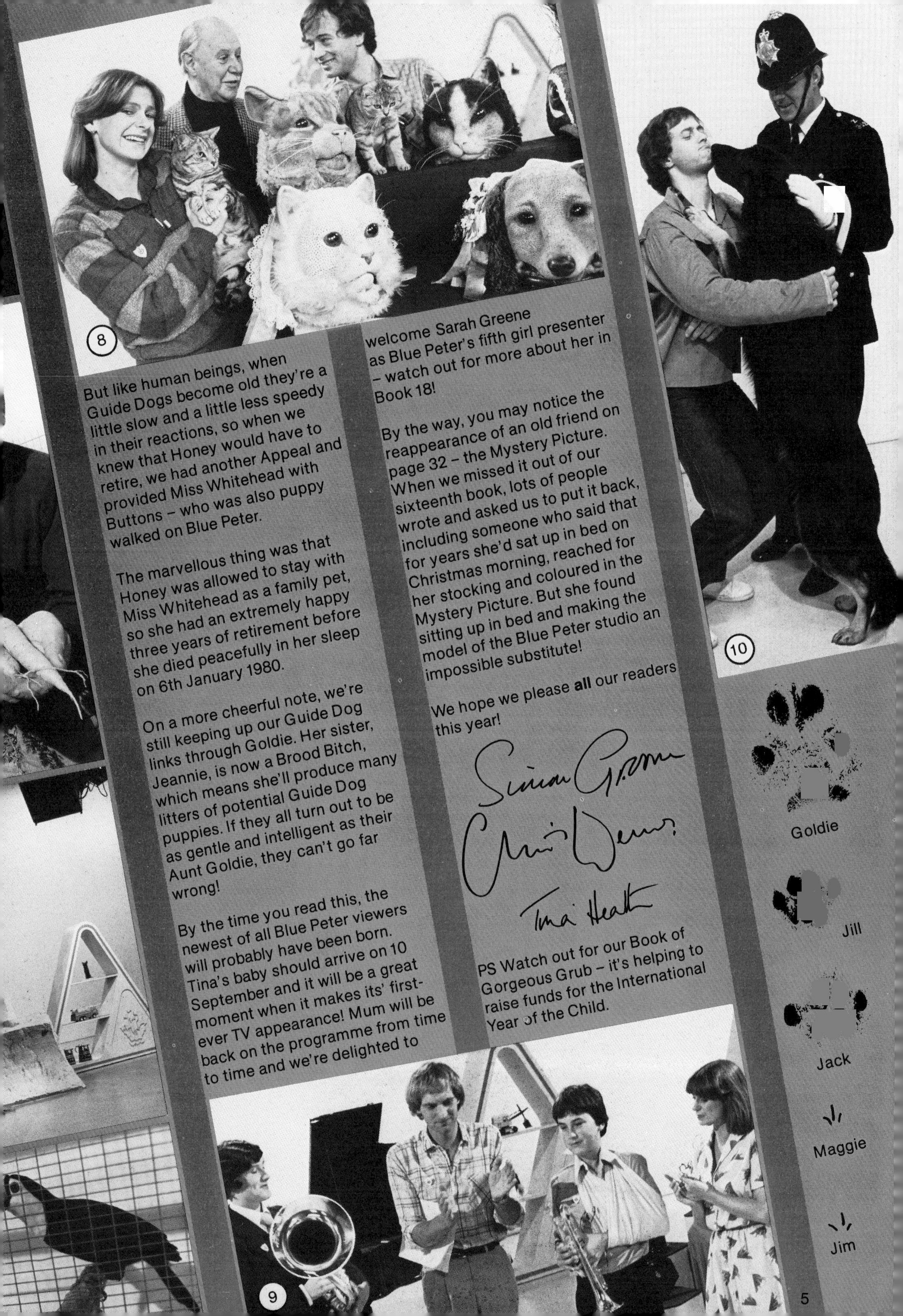

But like human beings, when Guide Dogs become old they're a little slow and a little less speedy in their reactions, so when we knew that Honey would have to retire, we had another Appeal and provided Miss Whitehead with Buttons – who was also puppy walked on Blue Peter.

The marvellous thing was that Honey was allowed to stay with Miss Whitehead as a family pet, so she had an extremely happy three years of retirement before she died peacefully in her sleep on 6th January 1980.

On a more cheerful note, we're still keeping up our Guide Dog links through Goldie. Her sister, Jeannie, is now a Brood Bitch, which means she'll produce many litters of potential Guide Dog puppies. If they all turn out to be as gentle and intelligent as their Aunt Goldie, they can't go far wrong!

By the time you read this, the newest of all Blue Peter viewers will probably have been born. Tina's baby should arrive on 10 September and it will be a great moment when it makes its' first-ever TV appearance! Mum will be back on the programme from time to time and we're delighted to welcome Sarah Greene as Blue Peter's fifth girl presenter – watch out for more about her in Book 18!

By the way, you may notice the reappearance of an old friend on page 32 – the Mystery Picture. When we missed it out of our sixteenth book, lots of people wrote and asked us to put it back, including someone who said that for years she'd sat up in bed on Christmas morning, reached for her stocking and coloured in the Mystery Picture. But she found sitting up in bed and making the model of the Blue Peter studio an impossible substitute!

We hope we please **all** our readers this year!

Simon Groom
Christopher Wenner
Tina Heath

PS Watch out for our Book of Gorgeous Grub – it's helping to raise funds for the International Year of the Child.

FLYING VISIT

The East Tower is, for us, the most important building at the Television Centre. It is the home not only of the Blue Peter Office, but of the whole of BBC Children's Programmes.

Most of the cutting rooms, dubbing theatres and preview theatres are there. Film from all over the world is screened every day, and reports are sent back to anxious crews on location in faraway places. "Your rushes are OK!" means you can press on with confidence, but terrible words like "edge fogging" and "under-exposed" may mean that the film is ruined and you have it all to do again.

The East Tower is the Headquarters of the BBC's Make-up Department where beards and wigs for BBC programmes are designed and made, and fitted on international stars and bit-part players alike.

The Documentary department is on the ninth floor, and every year at the beginning of December the Queen comes to the East Tower to finish off the Christmas Day broadcast.

Black-suited executives stalk the sixth floor, and ambitious young men in jeans rush about on the first and second, carrying cans of film and hoping one day to get to the top. The East Tower is full of ambitious young men, and I, too, wanted to get to the top. But being an impatient sort of chap, I decided to do it in a day – so I called in the Marines.

It's 60 metres from the road to the flat roof of the East Tower and the walls are sheer, with not so much as a finger-nail hold from top to bottom. But this was no problem for the Royal Marines. A long rope, a simple device called a lark's foot, attached to a handgrip called a dumar were all that Corporal Jan Rowe said we needed. What he didn't mention was that a right arm and right leg with the strength of Hercules would be useful additional requirements! The idea, Jan explained, was to pull yourself up on the dumar, taking your weight on your right arm whilst giving a little jump with your right leg. The lark's foot locks off on the rope which means you can't slide down again. The only snag is that you have to keep going forever upwards – and the twelfth floor seemed a very long way away!

Floating through the first window we reached I could hear *Barnacle Bill* – the Blue Peter signature tune — being played backwards. It was the Blue Peter cutting room and inside Mike and Frances were hard at work on the following Monday's film. Next week, I thought, they'll be working on the film of me climbing past their cutting-room window! There are 22 cutting-rooms in the East Tower. Next door I could hear the voice of Tucker Jenkins cheeking the Headmaster of Grange Hill. Next door to that Roy Castle was breaking records in Hawaii, and further down the corridor a voice was saying: "This is a house, this is a door – windows one, two, three, four . . ."

A few more heaves and a few more jumps and I swung past Tony Hart and Morph on the fourth floor, until on the floor above them I saw – no, not Oggy stamping about, but Biddy Baxter, the Blue Peter Editor, dictating a letter to Annie, her secretary. Tina was there, too, dealing with some of your letters, and John Adcock was on the telephone to New York. He's the man in charge of all the Blue Peter films, so I thought I'd better not hang around in case he thought I was slacking(!) The sixth floor is where the Head of Children's Programmes has his office, so I shot past there very quickly! But on the floor above I came face to face with a hideous monster. It really gave me a nasty turn, which I suppose is what it was meant to do because I was looking in on the *Dr Who* office whilst they were trying

out their latest spine-chiller. I normally watch *Dr Who* with a cushion to put over my eyes when it gets too frightening, but now I had no cushion, and no hands to spare, anyway! However, once the mask was removed it revealed a friendly face who asked us in for a cup of tea. I must admit I leapt at the chance, not only because I wanted to try on the monster mask, but because my right arm and right leg were killing me! They very kindly gave us a cup of *Dr Who* tea which was very welcome, but Jan said we ought to be on our way because the lads were waiting for us on the roof. It was then that I had a great idea. "You carry on up the outside, and I'll go up the stairs and join you at the top!" I know I was chickening out, but my muscles were telling me that seven floors were enough for the first go.

The Royal Marines didn't design dumars for Blue Peter presenters to climb up the East Tower. Normally they are used for walking up steep glaciers, or climbing up sheer clefts in the rock. Jan told me that this was the highest climb he'd ever attempted on dumars and it could be a world record.

"I wish you'd mentioned that on the seventh floor," I said, "because that was where the *Record Breakers* office is, and we might have got ourselves in the *Guinness Book of Records!*"

I rejoined Jan on the roof and we set about planning our descent . . .

"That's the easy bit, Chris," he said. "All we do is kick off and abseil."

60 metres below, a tube train, looking like a dinky, rumbled past on the Metropolitan line.

"Ready?" asked Jan.

"Those lines are electric, aren't they?" I said, looking down.

"Yes, but I shouldn't worry. If anything went wrong, the fall would probably kill you!"

"Thanks a million!" I said, and stepped over the parapet.

"Right, now turn round. Brace your feet against the wall, Chris. Now slowly – very slowly – kick off."

It was the most marvellous sensation, kicking off the walls and roaring past the windows until you hit the next bit of concrete with the soles of your boots. As I shot past the twelfth floor I saw a pair of big, brown eyes I could even recognise at 20 miles per hour – lovely Maggie Philbin of *Swap Shop*.

"What are you doing?" she asked.

"Just hanging around, hoping to meet somebody famous," I replied.

"What a swinging idea!" she said.

"Not too ropey," I said, hopefully.

"No. Drop in and see me anytime," she said.

Two more kicks and I was standing next to Jan on the pavement. "That was great,Jan," I said when I got my breath back."Thank you very much."

From where we were standing, we could see the Westway Flyover curling down towards the West End, with the tower blocks of London through the haze.

"Is that the Post Office Tower?" he asked.

"It is," I said. "But I only climb television buildings. If you want to climb the Post Office Tower – go and tell it to the postmen!"

MAGGIE & JIM

HATCHED 27.8.74

How many other tortoises in Britain are called after the Prime Minister and the Leader of the Opposition? They were the names chosen by Blue Peter viewers when our new baby tortoises became the programme's pets on Election Day – 3 May 1979 – the day we showed two extraordinary 3D caricatures of Margaret Thatcher and James Callaghan, made out of cottonwool, foam rubber and fabric!

But Maggie and Jim had made their very first *appearance* on Blue Peter nearly five years previously, with the man who bred them from the eggs, College Lecturer, Bob Woolley of Leicester. Bob brought them to our studio in September 1974 when they were three weeks old and scarcely bigger than a 50 pence piece.

Maggie and Jim paid a return visit in October 1976, so they were quite used to the studio surroundings when Bob made us a present of them last year. in fact, they must have felt very much at home, because with all the 400 kilowatt TV lights blazing down, our studio frequently feels like an outsized vivarium – or a scorching hot North African beach where Maggie and Jim's ancestors were hatched!

Like Freda, our first Blue Peter tortoise that they replaced, Maggie and Jim are Mediterranean tortoises – although Freda was the Spur Thighed variety while Maggie and Jim are Hermanns. But Maggie and Jim were hatched in Britain by Bob, the offspring of two of his six tortoises, Tina and Toby.

Quite a lot of Blue Peter viewers write and tell us that their pets have laid eggs – that's not too unusual. The tricky business is hatching them and keeping the babies alive, and this is where Bob has an amazing record. He and his wife, Jean, have achieved a successful hatching every time the

3 weeks old and scarcely bigger than a 50p piece.

Tortoise expert Bob Woolley who gave us our new pets.

Six thousand viewers suggested names for our tortoises – Maggie and Jim led the field with the most votes!

tortoises have laid eggs, but rearing the babies takes an enormous amount of time and attention.

It's important that baby tortoises in this country are *not* allowed to hibernate. They just aren't big enough to have stored up enough food to keep them going during their long sleep. Bob told us this was how so many small tortoises met their death, and showed us a fool-proof test:

The weight/length hibernation ratio

1 Measure length in mm

98mm

2 Weigh in grams

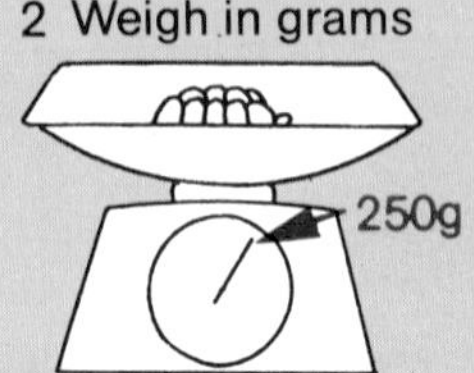

3 Divide length into weight (the little figure into the big figure)

250 ÷ 98 = 2.55

The answer is your tortoise's ratio. If it works out below 5 do not hibernate!

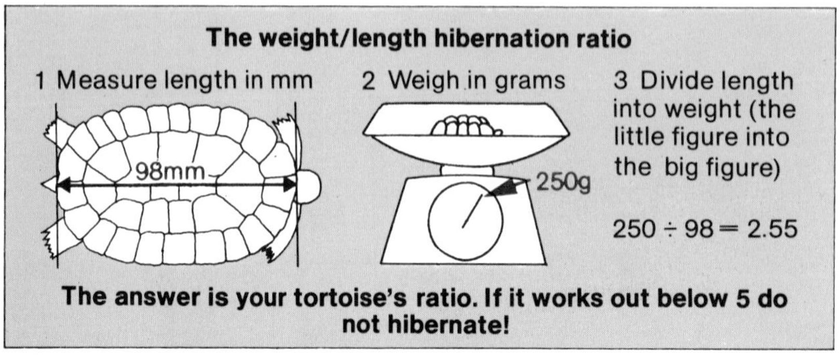

Do not let your tortoise hibernate unless he passes the weight/length ratio test.

If you're buying a tortoise from a shop, always insist on this weight and measure test – otherwise, you may have a tragic death on your hands. And if possible, try and find a home-bred tortoise that's bigger than 100 mm long. *Don't* buy one with a damaged shell, *or* one that looks sickly with running eyes or nose. Unscrupulous dealers import hundreds of thousands of Mediterranean tortoises and ship them to this country under the most inhumane conditions. If only people refused to buy tortoises that were obviously too young, this cruel practice would die out.

Bob showed us how to make a simple vivarium for Maggie and Jim – just a wooden box with a 40 watt bulb providing a steady temperature of 70°F. And he and Jean kept an eye on them for us during last winter.

Now they're back in the studio more lively than ever! They sprint across the floor like Sebastian Coe and very rarely stay in one place longer than a few seconds.

A few months ago, they met three tortoises belonging to Blue Peter viewers, whose joint lives added up to two hundred years. It's a sobering thought that Maggie and Jim could be appearing in front of the TV cameras long after the three of us are in our wheel chairs!

QUEEN MATILDA'S STRIP CARTOON

"1066 AND ALL THAT"

1066 is the one date in English history everyone knows – the year William the Conqueror came over from Normandy and defeated Harold at the Battle of Hastings and became the last foreign invader to conquer England. His conquest became the subject of the first strip cartoon in the world. We know it as the Bayeux Tapestry, although in France it is called the Tapestry of Queen Matilda, who was William's wife.

It is a piece of embroidery on a strip of coarse linen, seventy metres long and half a metre wide. Every stitch was put in more than nine hundred years ago, and yet it is as bright as the day it was made. It has always been treated with great care, and if you look at it closely, as I was able to, you can see where little holes have been mended by tiny darns, themselves centuries old.

An expert says the strip contains 626 human figures – 202 horses – 55 dogs – 505 other animals – 37 buildings – 41 ships and boats – and 49 trees. I wasn't in Bayeux long enough to check up for myself, but I am quite prepared to take their word for it!

It tells the story of William of Normandy's Conquest of England, from the Norman point of view. King Edward of England had promised William the throne of England when he died.

In 1064 King Edward sent his chief minister, Earl Harold, on a mission to William of Normandy. Harold set out by boat, taking his pet hawk on his wrist, but he was captured and made prisoner. William of Normandy was sent to rescue him, and treated him as an honoured guest.

But William made Harold swear an oath to support him as king when Edward died. Harold swore, under pressure, because he wanted to go home, but his hand had rested on the Holy relics from Bayeux Cathedral which meant the oath was too solemn ever to be broken.

Harold swore an oath of loyalty to support William as King when Edward died.

The Normans said a strange comet in the sky was a sign disaster would strike King Harold.

Harold went back to England, and on 5 January 1066 Edward died and was buried in the magnificent church he had built – it was Westminster Abbey. The nobles of England said they did not want William as their king – they asked Harold to rule over them, and he accepted. Then an extraordinary event took place. A strange comet was seen in the sky. It was Halley's comet, which can be seen from England about every 75 years. (Astronomers say we shall see it again in 1984.) When it appeared in 1066, the Normans said it was a sign a great disaster would strike King Harold.

When William heard Harold had accepted the Crown of England, he was furious. He called his nobles and told them he would invade England and claim the kingdom. He asked for their support and promised them all rich rewards.

They started building boats.

At Dives-sur-Mer, on the north coast of France, there is a column on the spot where William embarked for England. Today the harbour is silted up with sand, but it must have been a fantastic sight during the summer of 1066. William planned to take war horses to England by ship, as well as armed knights and foot soldiers. Some chroniclers say 3000 ships gathered at Dives, with 50,000 fighting men and 14,000 knights. William and his brother, the warlike Bishop Odo, were in command. Matilda gave money for a special ship for William – it was called the *Mora*.

At last they were ready – waiting for a favourable wind. And across the Channel, King Harold waited for the terrible invading army.

Suddenly, he heard dreadful news. His kingdom had been invaded –

William told his nobles he would claim the kingdom of England, and they built boats for the invasion.

The fleet crossed the channel. When the knights sighted England, they ran their ships up on the beach.

but by Norwegian forces from the North.

In an incredible march he took his army North, defeated the enemy – and *then* he had to turn round again and march south with his exhausted army. For weeks, Duke William had waited for a wind. At last it came, the longed-for south-west wind. Men, armour, provisions and horses were crammed into the boats. William led his knights down to the shore and set out across the waters of the Channel to invade England.

At last they sighted England. They ran their ships up on to the beach. The Duke, eager to lead his men, leapt out into the shallow water and rushed up the steep beach. He slipped on the shingle and fell. His men gasped in horror. This must be a bad omen. But William got up and laughed. He opened his clenched hands and showed them full of pebbles.

"Look, I have seized the soil of England in both my hands," he declared, and his men gave a mighty cheer.

William had a great piece of luck. The south coast was undefended while Harold and his army were defeating the invaders in the North, so all his men were able to land and bring ashore their horses at a place which, to this day, is called Norman's Bay. William moved along the coast, making his headquarters at Hastings. At last, the English and Norman armies met at a place which was ever afterwards called Battle, to begin the most important battle ever fought on English soil. The Normans were fighting for land and conquest – the English were defending their homeland – and both armies fought fiercely throughout a dreadful day.

William made Hastings his headquarters, and the place where the English and Norman armies had their first fight was later named "Battle".

Tradition says an arrow pierced King Harold's eye and Norman sword thrusts killed him.

Once the Normans thought William was wounded and had left the field. He raised the visor of his helmet to show them his face.

"Look, I am unharmed!" he shouted.

Towards evening, William ordered a great volley of arrows which fell on Harold, surrounded by his troops.

King Harold was wounded – tradition says an arrow pierced his eye – and Norman sword thrusts killed him. Then, says a chronicler, "the heart went out of the English and they yielded to William."

Then it is said that William buried Harold's body on the sea shore, and on a stone, wrote: "By command of the Duke you rest here a king, O Harold, that you may be guardian still of the shore and sea."

Now William Duke of Normandy was William the Conqueror, King of England.

Before the battle, he had sworn an oath to his troops: "Upon this place of battle I will found a monastery for the salvation of you all," and after his victory, he gave orders for building to start. So Battle Abbey was born, and stood for 500 years, and you can still visit its ruins today.

Ten weeks after the battle, on Christmas Day, 1066, William the Conqueror was crowned in Westminster Abbey – the first of a long line of Kings and Queens to be crowned in the Abbey.

Now the golden lions of Normandy floated over England, too, and they are still part of the royal coat of arms.

William was a harsh ruler, never loved in the land he made his own. He built strong castles all over the country, to put down any rising by his English subjects, and they too, still stand.

And William left another legacy, too.

He wanted to know the value of the land he had conquered, and which he shared out among his Norman barons. He sent questioners everywhere, village by village, asking how much land every man ploughed – how many oxen he owned – even how many beehives he possessed.

William called this survey "The Description of All England", but the English called it Domesday Book. The ordinary people were very alarmed. "Why does the king want to know if I own a pig?" they asked, but no one could escape the remorseless enquiry. Two great volumes were drawn up, and because of William's survey, we know more about England in the eleventh century than about any other country in Europe.

So William was ruler of England, and the royal line he established has lasted for more than 900 years – our present queen is 29th in line from William. He had crossed the Channel and invaded England. Centuries later, others tried – Philip of Spain with his Armada – Napoleon – then Hitler – but they all failed.

So 1066 – the year of the three kings – was a momentous year for England.

No wonder we all remember the date!

Now William the Conqueror was King of England.

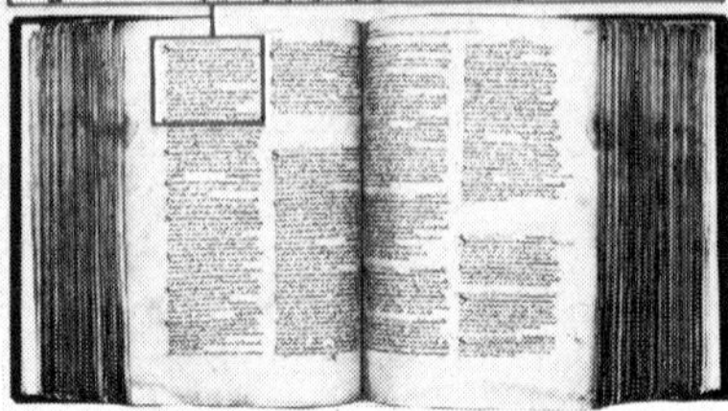

The 900-year-old Domesday Book is kept at the Public Record Office in London. When I went to see it, I was actually allowed to hold it in my hands.

SMASH HIT!

We had stacks of letters from Blue Peter viewers about Chris's journey in the steps of William the Conqueror. Some wanted to know exactly how Queen Elizabeth II is 29th in line from William I. One school wanted us to visit Waltham Abbey, near them, which King Harold founded – and a great many people wanted to know more about the Bayeux Tapestry.

And we had a phone call from Mr Wall of Mirfield, in Yorkshire, who told us that one of his most precious possessions was a Bayeux Tapestry plate. Very kindly, he said he would send it to us to look at.

But when it arrived at the Blue Peter office, the plate was in smithereens – smashed to pieces in its parcel. You can imagine how dreadful we felt when we opened it.

We told this sad story on the programme, and showed the broken pieces.

But Blue Peter viewers came to the rescue again, and as soon as we were off the air, we had calls from people offering to mend the plate. One came from Mr David Salmon, who specialises in the craft of repairing broken china. He said he would put the plate together for us. So we handed over the broken pieces, thinking we'd given him a very hard task.

Meanwhile we discovered the plate was made about 1910, by Doulton, and it was one of a set of three Bayeux Tapestry plates.

Then – after some weeks – David Salmon sent us the plate back. It was incredible! We could hardly believe our eyes. Not only did the plate look absolutely perfect from the front - even on the back there were no signs of glue, or cracks in the glaze. It was like magic. It really was as good as the day it was made – seventy years ago!

You can be sure we packed up the plate with the greatest care, and we were very relieved when we heard from Mr Wall that it had reached Mirfield safely.

China restorer, David Salmon – the man with the magic fingers.

K9 KRUNCH

If you're like me and you have a dog or a puppy, you'll have noticed it's becoming increasingly expensive to buy dog food. Years ago, people gave their dogs left-overs instead of pricey tinned food and found it just as good – and so does Goldie today. But dogs *do* like a really hard biscuit to chew on, and these two recipes sent in by Blue Peter viewers certainly fit the bill. Cats seem to like them, too, judging by Jack and Jill, and even if you don't have a dog or a cat of your own, you could make these biscuits for Sales of Work, or for an elderly person who can't afford to buy pet food. They're both excellent recipes, but we found Mrs Meyer's the simpler.

Falkirk biscuits

Sent to us by Mrs Meyer of Falkirk, who started making them because dog biscuits in the local shops had been in short supply.

Ingredients:
Equal amounts of wholewheat and plain flour (we used 175g. (6 oz.) of each); a little bacon fat or sausage fat; chopped bacon rinds; stale grated cheese; left-over meat scraps; gravy or cold water.

Method:

1 Put both lots of flour into the mixing bowl. Warm the fat to make it easy to pour, add it to the flour and rub well in.

2 Add the bacon rinds, grated cheese and any meaty left-over scraps. Mix well.
3 Add gravy or cold water and mix until the mixture becomes a fairly firm dough.

4 Put the dough onto a floured pastry board. Sprinkle some flour onto your rolling pin and onto the dough to prevent sticking. Roll the dough out to about ½ cm (or ¼″) thick.

5 Cut the dough into fingers or into small shapes, using a pastry cutter.

6 Put the biscuits onto a well-greased (or non-stick) baking tray. Place the tray on the middle shelf of the oven and cook slowly for several hours on gas mark 2, 300 F or 150 C electric.
7 Remove from oven when crisp and hard. Leave to cool.

York biscuits

Miss Hutchinson of York told us she started making these biscuits for the pets on the camp when she was a cook in the W.A.A.F. during the Second World War.

Ingredients:
125 g (4 oz) self-raising flour
25 g (1 oz) oatmeal or rolled oats
25 g (1 oz) dripping
50 g (2 oz) meat scraps or left-overs
1 tablespoon olive oil
Gravy

Method:
1 Put flour, oats and dripping into a mixing bowl and rub together.
2 Add the meat, olive oil and gravy and mix to a stiff dough.
3 Roll out the dough, cut and cook in exactly the same way as for the Falkirk biscuits.

PS Cats like them too!

CURTAIN UP!

Little did we guess when we invited the cast of the TV series *The Swish of the Curtain* to appear on the programme last April that one of them was going to be our new presenter!

"Swish" was Sarah Greene's first big TV role but she seemed so at home in the Blue Peter studio, the Editor asked her to audition for us.

After that things really moved fast! In less than three weeks from her audition, Sarah was rushed to Cornwall to make two films, and the following Monday she made her debut on the programme.

"The hardest part of being asked to join the team was keeping it secret until the day of my first programme. My eight–year–old sister's a firm fan – she's actually won a Blue Peter badge – I didn't dare tell her the good news in advance – I think she might have burst!"

A scene from "The Swish of the Curtain" – me and the other members of the Blue Door Theatre Company.

Tina showed me some of the 4,000 letters that reach the Blue Peter office each week.

When we were asked to take part in Blue Peter I never dreamt that I was going to be the new presenter.

HEROES OF THE SKIES

"Forward 20 yards – 15 yards – 10 yards – Easy – Easy – Steady – Clear to go down – 15 feet – 10 feet – 5 feet – "

A huge Wessex Royal Naval helicopter inched its way down to the VIP car park at the Television Centre, missing the lamp posts on either side by a whisker.

No, it wasn't the arrival of the Director General. It was the men and women of Culdrose Naval Air Station coming to collect our first Blue Peter Award for Outstanding Endeavour.

It was Christopher Trace, the first male presenter on Blue Peter, who came up with the idea of an Award. During our 20th Birthday celebrations, Christopher said he'd like to donate a solid bronze medallion, engraved with our Blue Peter ship, to be awarded each year for a feat of Outstanding Endeavour.

We drew up a short list before we went on our summer holidays, and then on 14 August 1979, the Atlantic gales blew up a storm which shattered the holidays of millions of people and left us with only one name on our paper.

The great Fastnet Yacht Race from Cowes over to Ireland and back to Plymouth had begun a few days earlier in clear blue skies, but the treacherous August gales which once shattered the Spanish Armada, turned this sporting event into a tragedy. 300 yachts were in peril in near-hurricane force winds and raging seas with waves higher than houses. Immediately the helicopter crews of Culdrose raced to the rescue, and as the hours went by it was apparent that an awful disaster was at hand. When the News Bulletins broadcast the details, crew members on leave rushed back to Culdrose to join their comrades in the rescue.

During the next two days, twelve helicopters flew non-stop making rescues in the horrendous conditions. They flew a total of 194 hours and 15 minutes, and

The dramatic Fastnet rescue involved everyone at Culdrose from the medical unit and the ground crew to the fire brigade and the cooks.

While Chris was having dinghy drill I met the chopper crew – Martin Cox, the winchman, Jamie Bauld, the diver, and Alby Fox, the pilot.

All at sea ...

... Scramble ...

... Lift off ...

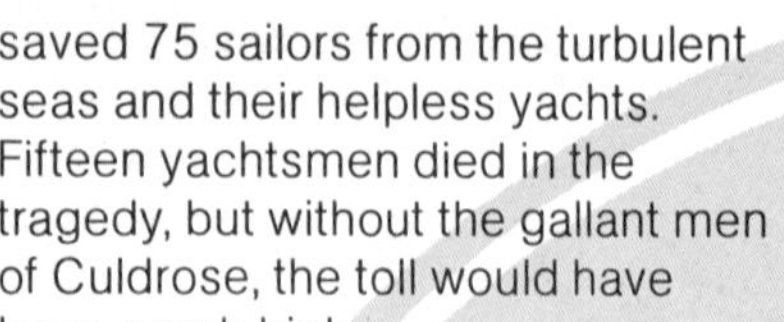

saved 75 sailors from the turbulent seas and their helpless yachts. Fifteen yachtsmen died in the tragedy, but without the gallant men of Culdrose, the toll would have been much higher.

When the crews came to the Blue Peter studio to collect their Award, we were invited to find out at first hand exactly what's involved in a helicopter air-sea rescue.

The idea was for Christopher to be the victim who'd be winched up into the helicopter from the sea whilst I flew with the crew on the mission. We were in safe hands! All three were heroes of the Fastnet disaster. Lieutenant Alby Fox, Leading Air Crewman Martin Cox, and Chief Air Crewman Jamie Bauld had all worked as part of the Culdrose Search and Rescue team, flying in gruelling 4-hour shifts on their life-saving mission.

Before either Chris or I could fly, we had to go through several briefings. We learnt how to operate our life-saving equipment, what we had to do if the chopper crashed into the sea, and how to get in and out of the "strop" that hauls you up into the helicopter.

Then we split up. I went to the crew room to await the training "emergency" while Chris went out to sea.

Off the Cornish coast he was dumped in a dinghy and left to fend for himself. As instructed, he let off a bright orange smoke flare that could be seen for miles.

The rescue operation had begun!

The Lizard Coastguard spotted the signal.

The phone shrilled in the Crew Duty Room at Culdrose. "Scramble!" yelled the Coastguard Liaison Officer and the crew raced across the tarmac to the waiting helicopter.

It took just 2½ minutes from the call to being airborne. As Alby Fox skimmed low over the Cornish fields, Martin Cox, the winchman, and Jamie Bauld, the diver, prepared for action. Jamie told me his job was to go down on the winch and pull the victims out of the sea, while Martin controlled the winch and gave Alby instructions over the intercom. When a chopper is above the victim, the pilot can't see what is happening, so he has to rely on the expertise of the winchman to talk him into position.

Meanwhile, back at Culdrose our "scramble" was receiving priority treatment. Chief Medical Assistant Traylor alerted the Sick Bay, and John Gerrell packed an Emergency Doctor's kit and dashed to a waiting ambulance outside to meet the chopper on its return. The Galley was alerted, too, so that food could be prepared for the victim. Hot soup can be a life saver!

In the Operations Room our position was plotted as we moved near to the rescue zone. We were now within sight of Chris and I could just see his fluorescent orange raft bobbing in the sea. As we moved closer in, Martin began giving instructions to the pilot. "15 yards to run – Speed good – 10 yards – 5 yards – Easy – Easy – Steady – On top of survivor – Strop in hand – Placing strop round his back – Attached to winch – Line plumb – Up 10 feet – "

Below us I could see Chris being gathered up from a calm, flat sea. I thought how different it must have been for Jamie on those terrible August days, blown by Force 10 gales and plunging into mountainous seas. On 15 and 16 August, Jamie rescued 14 men, working non-stop throughout, as did the ten other divers from Culdrose.

Winchman Martin Cox hauled Chris up as Alby Fox held the Wessex steady: "Raising the winch – coming up level the steps – bringing him in – unhooking – checking them out."

Seventy-five yachtsmen had reached safety like this. And the men and women of Culdrose received fourteen citations and awards for their bravery.

Culdrose decided to set their Blue Peter Award in a granite plinth where it could be seen by all their visitors. Next to it, a letter from the Prime Minister reads:

". . . The whole country salutes the skills and courage of those who took part in the rescue."

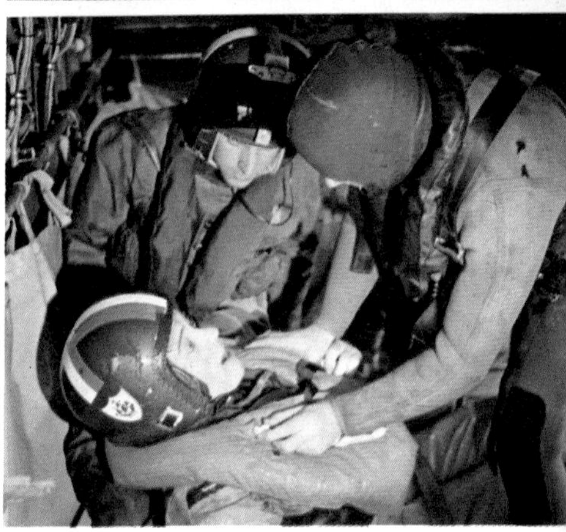

Another exercise successfully over. It's training like this that makes the men and women of Culdrose admired all over the world.

PADDINGTON'S CHRISTMAS TREASURE HUNT

Story by Michael Bond illustrated by "Hargreaves"

Mrs Brown opened the kitchen window of number thirty-two Windsor Gardens and gazed out with a puzzled expression on her face.
"That's very strange,"she said. "Fancy hearing a bumble-bee at this time of the year. It's only two weeks to Christmas."

Mrs Bird joined her at the sink and cupped one hand to her ear. Sure enough, the quiet of the afternoon was suddenly broken into by a loud buzzing noise. If it was a bumble-bee it was certainly one which was suffering from the effects of the weather, for every so often the buzz developed into a spluttering wheeze, followed by an ominous silence as if it was gathering its second wind before continuing a fruitless search for the last rose of summer.

For a moment or two the Browns' housekeeper looked as puzzled as Mrs Brown. Then, as her sharp eyes caught a movement behind some shrubs, followed by a momentary glimpse of a familiar-looking blue duffle-coat, her face cleared.

"That's not a bumble-bee," she said, as she returned to her baking. "That's Paddington. He must be having another look for buried treasure with Mr Brown's Magic-probe."

"Is that all?" Mrs Brown looked relieved as she closed the window. Mrs Bird's remark had solved two problems which had been bothering her. One was the noise of the "bee"; the other was the lack of noise from Paddington. Mrs Brown always felt uneasy when Paddington was quiet for long at a time. It usually meant he was "up to something".

"All the same," she glanced out of the window again, "I do hope he's wrapped up well. We don't want him in bed with a cold over Christmas."

"Hmm!" Mrs Bird gave a snort. "I doubt if he'll be out there very long. Too many people have been over the ground before. I'll match Paddington's weight in marmalade against any treasure he finds buried."

Having made her pronouncement Mrs Bird went back to work with the air of one confident that her predictions would come true. In saying that the garden at number thirty-two Windsor Gardens had been "gone over", the Browns' housekeeper was speaking from practical experience, for she had been one of the first to join in the general excitement when Mr Brown received a metal detector for his birthday.

In the event the "Magic-probe" had proved something of a nine-days' wonder. Apart from a few old tools which had lain buried over the years, the garden had yielded very little in the way of objects of value, and after Paddington had dug up a telephone cable by mistake one morning the detector had been put into cold storage by general consent to await better weather and the prospect of trips to the sea-side.

"Not," said Mrs Bird, "that I wouldn't put it past that bear to come up with something. He has the luck of Old Nick."

Unaware that he was the object of some discussion in the kitchen, Paddington settled himself down behind the raspberry canes and gazed disconsolately at a small booklet he held in his paw.

It was called EVERY MAN A TREASURE ISLAND and it was written by a Mr Arnold Prosper. The picture on the front cover showed Mr Prosper dressed in Elizabethan costume clutching one of his probes like a buccaneer fresh from doing battle with the Spanish Fleet and surrounded by the spoils of battle.

According to the foreword, most people, if they did but know it, were standing on something of value. Doubloons sovereigns, items of bronze, silver and other precious metals; Mr Prosper had amassed so much during his career he had a job to squeeze them all into the many photographs in his book. Looking at his own "spoils" – several rusty nails, an old bicycle pedal and a horseshoe – Paddington had to admit he would have been hard put to fill a postage stamp let alone anything larger.

Heaving a deep sigh he opened his suitcase and turned his attention to a glossy pamphlet which he withdrew from the secret compartment. Paddington was very keen on brochures and he often sent away for them. They were a good way of finding out about things and over the years he'd formed a large collection. But this particular one was unsolicited and had arrived through the post several days before. Most of one side was taken up by a picture of a cake; but not just any old cake – a very unusual kind called AUNTIE MABEL'S PECAN NUT SPECIAL.

According to the wording on the back, Auntie Mabel and her team of willing helpers had been hard at work for some months baking them ready for the coming holiday season. And if the number of glowing testimonials from satisfied customers who'd ordered them the year before was anything to go by, no Christmas could possibly be complete without one.

With Christmas not far away Paddington was already well into his shopping, but not for the first time he was at a loss to know what to buy the BLUE PETER team. BLUE PETER had always been rather a problem. Over the years his circle of friends on the programme had grown and grown, and although he was a generous bear at heart it had become impossible to buy each and every one of them a present.

A cake had seemed like a very good idea indeed. Looking at the picture again Paddington felt sure that with careful slicing they could all have one if not two pieces for Christmas tea.

Unfortunately, like all good things in life there was a price to pay, and although Auntie Mabel was at pains to point out that with the cost of pecan nuts going up all the time, ten pounds – including postage and packing – was a mere trifle, it was far beyond Paddington's means. His Christmas savings had already been severely dented following a bout of present buying for the Brown family, and they were in very definite need of an injection of ready cash.

The need for prompt action had caused him to pay a visit to his friend Mr Gruber, who kept an antique shop in the Portobello Road. Mr Gruber was always willing and able to give advice on practically every subject under the sun, and once again he'd turned up trumps. From among the many books lining his shelves he'd produced an A – Z on unusual careers.

Unfortunately however, like many of his books, its value lay in its age and most of the jobs covered belonged to more leisured times. Having rejected in quick succession possible careers in Bath Management, Deep Sea Diving and Lighthouse Keeping – all of which seemed to need long periods of training – Paddington had been about to give up when he'd caught sight of a section on Gold Prospecting, and this in turn had reminded him of Mr Brown's Magic-probe.

Returning to the instruction book, Paddington leafed through a section at the end where, in a series of pictures, Mr Prosper made the point that some of his best finds had come about largely by accident. One photograph even showed him tossing a coin over his shoulder in order to mark the spot for his next "dig". Three pictures later, dressed this time as Long John Silver with a parrot on his shoulder, he was shown holding up a large silver plate worth, so the caption said, several hundred pounds.

Closing his eyes, Paddington lay back amongst the raspberries and tried to picture the scene. Despite the time of year, the search for buried treasure had made him feel quite hot. So much so, he loosened one of the toggles on his duffle-coat as he rested his head against one of the canes. As his paw dropped limply to the ground he felt it come up against something cold and hard, and gradually an idea floated into his mind.

If Arnold Prosper had achieved so much success simply by throwing a coin over his shoulder, who could tell what would happen with something really big; something as large as a horseshoe for example. It was the kind of thought which was difficult to resist, especially with matters reaching such a desperate stage.

Paddington was a hopeful bear at heart, but even he hadn't bargained on quite such a speedy result from his action – or such a noisy one.

The horseshoe hardly seemed to have left his paw when the air was torn asunder by a loud yell from somewhere close at hand.

"Bear!" came the familiar voice of the Browns' next-door neighbour, Mr Curry. "Did you do that, bear?"

At first glance Mr Curry looked as if he had become inextricably attached to a pneumatic drill that had run amok, for he was bobbing up and down on the other side of the fence like someone on a pogo stick. But closer inspection through a knot hole revealed that in fact he was hopping around on one leg, clutching his other foot with both hands, his face getting redder and redder with every passing moment.

"Did you do that, bear?" he repeated, pointing a trembling finger at the offending horseshoe. "Because, if so . . ."

"Oh no, Mr Curry," explained Paddington, anxious to make amends. "I didn't actually *do* it. It just happened. Besides," he added brightly, as a sudden thought struck him. "Mrs Bird always says horseshoes are supposed to be lucky."

"Lucky!" bellowed Mr Curry. "*Lucky?*" He paused in his antics. "I don't call having a great lump of iron land on my foot lucky. I've a very good mind to . . ."

The Browns' neighbour broke off as he looked over the fence and caught sight of the various items of equipment lying on the ground where Paddington had left them.

"What have you got there, bear?" he demanded suspiciously.

"That's Mr Brown's Magic-probe, Mr Curry," said Paddington, only too pleased to change the subject. "I'm looking for treasure."

"Treasure?" Mr Curry hobbled closer to the fence in order to take a closer look. "What sort of treasure?"

"Oh, all sorts," exclaimed Paddington, warming to his subject. "Buried especially." He picked up the instruction book, which as luck would have it was still open at the page where Mr Prosper had found his silver plate. "That's why I threw the horseshoe – I wanted to see where to start my next sweep."

"Hmm." Mr Curry considered the matter for a moment or two, then he marched to the centre of the lawn and indicated the bedraggled remains of a flower bed which he'd just started to dig.

"Well, I suggest you start right now. If you manage to find anything – which I very much doubt, I *may* not report you for your dangerous behaviour just now."

Paddington needed no second bidding. Without so much as a backward glance towards the house he picked up his belongings and before the Browns' neighbour had a chance to change his mind, pushed aside some loose boards in the fence.

Although it was true to say that Mrs Bird thought highly of the lucky properties of horseshoes, she held equally strong views on the subject of those who threw things without looking first, and he had no wish to be reported – especially with Christmas so near at hand.

"Right." Mr Curry pointed to a dent in the ground where he was standing. "That's where it landed."

Paddington eyed the spot doubtfully as he began setting up his equipment. He'd seldom seen a less inviting patch of ground. Apart from a few earth worms who seemed relieved to be able to make good their escape now the soil had been turned over, it looked so barren even Mr Prosper might have been tempted to have another go with his coin.

"Perhaps you'd like to go indoors and wait while I make my search, Mr Curry?" he suggested hopefully.

The Browns' neighbour glared at him. "I shall do no such thing, bear!" he barked. "There's no knowing what sort of tricks you'd get up to once my back was turned."

"*Tricks*, Mr Curry?" Paddington looked most offended as he pressed the switch on Mr Brown's Magic-probe.

"Yes, bear, *tricks*." The Browns' neighbour looked as if he was about to compile a long list of things which might happen if Paddington was left to his own devices, but before he had a chance to make a start his words were drowned by a loud rasping noise from the probe.

"Good heavens!" he exclaimed. "What was that?"

Paddington looked equally astonished. "I don't know, Mr Curry," he said excitedly. "I think it must be something very valuable indeed."

In his book of instructions Arnold Prosper had listed the various sounds the probe made whenever it came within range of any buried metal, so that a skilled operator could soon learn to tell the difference between worthless junk and items of value. But nowhere had he seen any mention of quite such a loud noise. Mr Prosper's noises ranged between the soft murmur of a gnat on a summer's day and a comb and paper, whereas the present one sounded more like a motor cycle that had gone wildly out of control during a TT race.

Switching it on again, he moved towards the spot where Mr Curry was standing. Immediately the rasping grew louder, until by the time he was directly over Mr Curry's feet it threatened to blow the very cone out of the loudspeaker, and he had to quickly turn the volume down.

Mr Curry's eyes nearly popped out of his head. "I take back all I said, bear," he remarked grudgingly. Then he looked round carefully to make sure no one else could overhear. "We must keep this a secret – just between the two of us. We'll go shares on anything we find."

Paddington's face fell. Mr Curry's meanness was legendary in the neighbourhood, out-weighed only by his bad-temper, and from past experience he knew that any sharing would be very one-sided indeed.

But in the event whatever decision he might have come to would have mattered little, for the Browns' neighbour was already hard at work with his spade.

"Keep your eyes peeled, bear," he growled. "We don't want any interruptions. If you see anyone watching tell them to mind their own business."

"Yes, Mr Curry." Glad to be left to his own devices for a while, Paddington stood back and watched as the pile of earth grew larger and larger. Every so often, at Mr Curry's request, he switched on the probe and waved it to and fro across the spot where he was digging, and each time there was an answering buzz. If it didn't get any louder – which was scarcely possible – it certainly didn't get any less.

"Are you sure that thing's working properly?" gasped Mr Curry some while later, as he climbed out of the hole and stood mopping his brow like some early gold prospector in the grip of the fever.

"Oh, yes, Mr Curry," said Paddington. And to prove the matter beyond all doubt he demonstrated over the horseshoe which had started it all, and which now lay forgotten on the nearby lawn.

"Hmmm." The Browns' neighbour looked round at the gathering dusk and then came to a decision. "I'm going indoors to fetch a torch, bear," he announced. "I'm not giving up now. While I'm gone you can carry on with the digging. But as soon as you find anything," he warned, "stop immediately. I don't want you putting your spade through anything valuable."

As Mr Curry disappeared up the garden path Paddington lowered himself gently into the hole. It was a large hole – almost up to his shoulders, and he could quite see why Mr Curry looked so worn out. Reaching up for the Magic-probe, he decided to have one last quick check before he started work, but as he switched it on a worried expression came over his face.

Gone was the loud rasping sound of a few moments before. In its place was the familiar low-pitched burr which showed that the machine was working, but nothing more.

He tried switching it on and off several times, but all to no avail, and even turning the volume up and shaking it produced nothing more than a few crackles.

Paddington gazed in growing alarm, first at the end of the probe and then at the bottom of the hole. Mr Curry's treasure seemed to have vanished into thin air. Worse still, before he had time to investigate the matter there came a tramping of feet and the Browns' neighbour arrived back on the scene.

"Bear!" he barked. "Why aren't you digging, bear?"

"I was just about to, Mr Curry," cried Paddington, blinking in the light from the torch. "Except there's no need to now. At least . . ." he broke off as simultaneously with the

Magic-probe bursting into life again he caught sight of something – a momentary gleam – which made his stomach turn to water.

"No need to?" bellowed Mr Curry. "What do you mean – there's no need to?" He stared down at Paddington. "What's up, bear? Is anything the matter? And what are you doing – waving that thing about in the air? The treasure's under *your* feet – not mine."

"I don't think so, Mr Curry," said Paddington mournfully, as the awful truth dawned on him. "I think we've been getting signals from your studs."

"My *studs?*" repeated Mr Curry. "What studs?"

"The studs on your boots," said Paddington. "That's why it always sounded as if the treasure was under your feet no matter how deep down you went. Mr Prosper says you have to watch out for these things. If you look in the instruction book . . ." He broke off from his explanations as a gasp of strangled rage came from somewhere overhead. Even without the aid of the torch the look on Mr Curry's face would have been frightening to behold; caught in the rays as he waved it to and fro it was positively menacing.

"Bear!" he bellowed. "Bear. . ."

Paddington wasn't sure what happened next. His feet felt like lead as he tried to scramble out of the hole in order to escape, but try as he might he couldn't gain a foothold. Above it all was the loud buzzing of the probe together with the sound of voices, and then . . .

"Paddington!" Mrs Brown's voice came to him through the haze. "Paddington! What *are* you doing? We wondered where on earth you'd got to."

"Fancy going to sleep in the garden at this time of the year," said Judy, shining her torch on him. "You'll catch your death of cold."

"And Dad won't be too pleased if you wear out his batteries," said Jonathan, reaching down to switch off the Magic-probe.

As the noise stopped Paddington stood up and rubbed his eyes. "I think," he announced to the world in general, "I've been having a daymare."

"That's the same as a nightmare," he explained, "only much, much worse. Especially when it's about Mr Curry."

"Well," said Mrs Bird, "if the noise you were making and the way you were jumping about was anything to go by, I for one believe you."

"I was trying to climb out of Mr Curry's hole, Mrs Bird," said Paddington. "I'd been looking for buried treasure – only it suddenly disappeared."

"Treasure," said Mrs Bird sternly, "buried or otherwise, has a habit of doing just that. You don't often get something for nothing in this world. However," she took hold of Paddington's paw and led him up the path towards the house, "be that as it may, you woke just in time."

Paddington knew better than to ask questions, but as they arrived in the kitchen and the Browns' housekeeper opened the oven door he nearly fell over backwards with surprise, for there in front of him, moist and glistening and golden brown, was an enormous cake.

"It's made of pecan nuts," said Judy, as she helped Mrs Bird lift it from the oven. "Not only that, but it's shaped just like a BLUE PETER badge."

Paddington could hardly believe his eyes and he pinched himself several

times in order to make sure he wasn't still dreaming. It really was uncanny the way Mrs Bird "knew" about things.

"I happened to come across your cake brochure," she explained, reading Paddington's thoughts. "It looked too good to resist."

"And then a certain person who keeps an antique shop not a million miles from here happened to mention your Christmas present problem," added Jonathan, "so we all got together."

Paddington sniffed the air happily. Good though Auntie Mabel's Pecan Nut Specials undoubtedly were, he was sure they wouldn't have stood a chance in competition with Mrs Bird's, and were he to be armed with one of his most sensitive probes, even Arnold Prosper would have been hard put to locate anything more delicious. It certainly more than made up for all he'd been through with Mr Curry in his daymare.

He licked his lips. "I think," he announced, amid laughter, "I'd better take it to the BLUE PETER studio myself. After all, it's a bit difficult cutting a cake for so many people and they may need some help!"

"Stand by Studio ...3 ...2 ...1 ...We're on the Air!"

Every Monday and Thursday our Studio Director cues Mike Oldfield's version of our signature tune and Blue Peter appears "live" all over the United Kingdom. But before that moment, up to 50 people have been working flat out, starting at . . . .

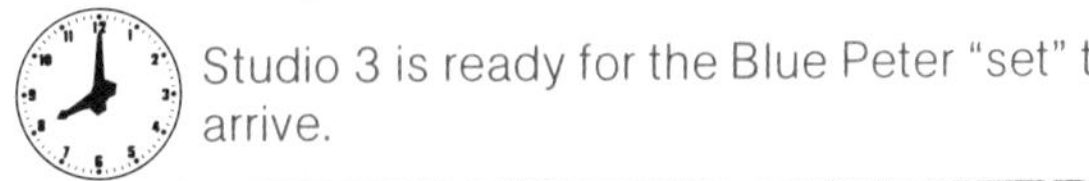

Studio 3 is ready for the Blue Peter "set" to arrive.

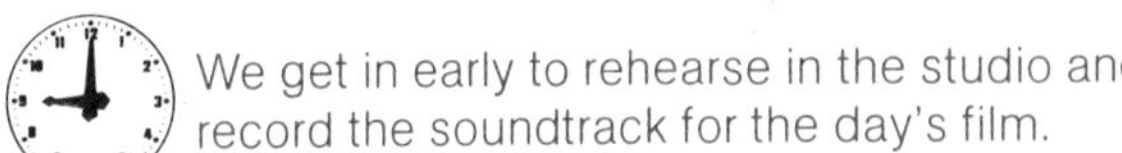

We get in early to rehearse in the studio and record the soundtrack for the day's film.

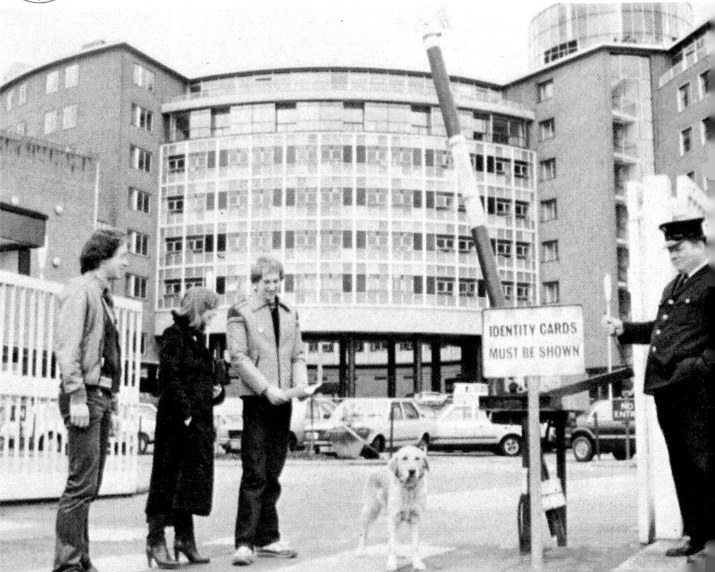

The scene crew pull and stretch a white curtain called a cyclorama to cover up the bare studio walls.

Members of Crew 4 begin plugging in the cameras and wheeling out the pedestals to fix them on. On Blue Peter we use five different cameras. They're not always mounted on pedestals. We use cranes for especially high shots.

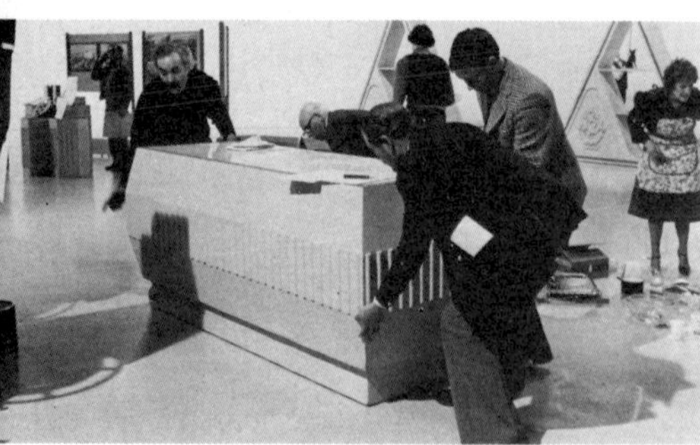

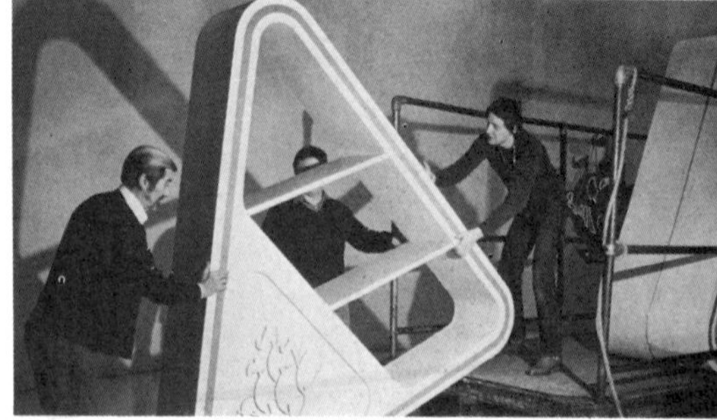

Our shelves, tables and seats arrive by truck and the blue perspex ship is hung by wire from the studio roof.

The electricians begin arranging the 250 lamps needed to light the Blue Peter set. Long poles are used to turn each lamp so that it's pointing the right way. Jeff, the Lighting Supervisor, uses a walkie-talkie to speak to his control room which is upstairs overlooking the studio. Each lamp can be individually controlled.

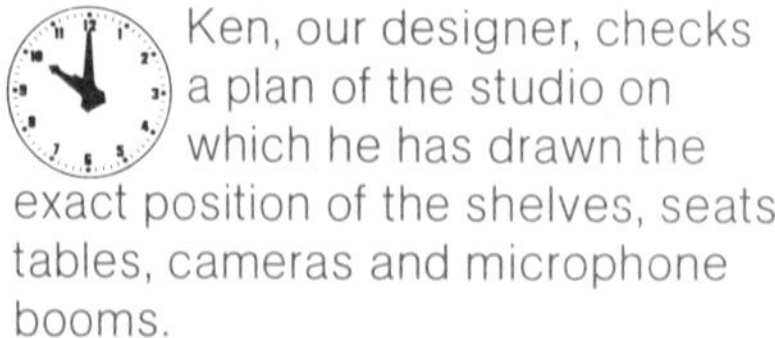

Ken, our designer, checks a plan of the studio on which he has drawn the exact position of the shelves, seats, tables, cameras and microphone booms.

Jack and Jill arrive in their travelling basket at TV Centre Reception. Edith Menezes (right) looks after them – and Maggie & Jim, too.

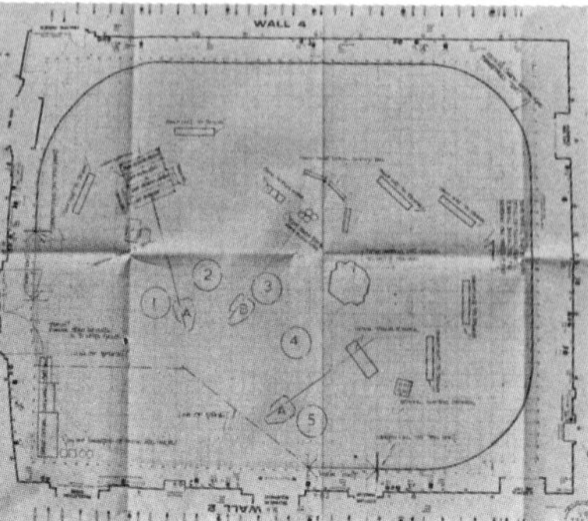

The microphones are tested on the studio floor, and upstairs, Martin, the Sound Supervisor, checks his dozens of faders to make sure everything's ready for rehearsals to start.

Now it's our turn. Chris Fox, our Floor Manager, relays all the Director's instructions from the Control room above. He uses arm and hand signals to tell us when to start and stop.

Margaret Parnell, who invents most of the things we make, and Vivien, our AFM (Assistant Floor Manager) help to get the cookery item ready.

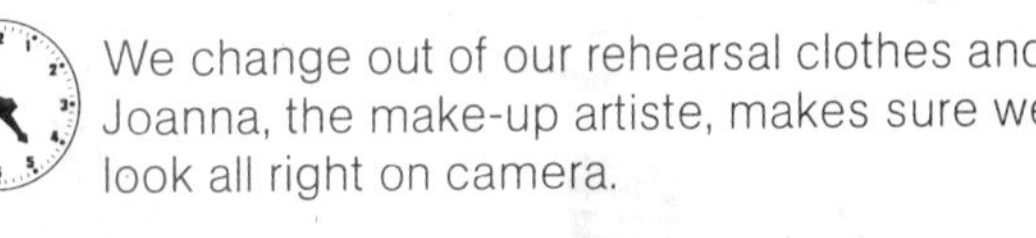

We change out of our rehearsal clothes and Joanna, the make-up artiste, makes sure we look all right on camera.

The Control room is the nerve centre of the Blue Peter studio. Here the Director, Frances, sits with her assistant and the vision mixer who presses the buttons that change the shots from one camera to another. The Technical Manager sits at the end making sure the programme "leaves" the studio and reaches you at home.

Stand by studio . . . 10 seconds to go . . . Run TK . . . Film running . . . 3 . . . 2 . . . 1 . . . Fade up . . . Superimpose "Blue Peter". . . Good luck studio . . . We're on the air!

EE-AYE-ADDIO-WE WON THE CUP!

How's your dribbling, shooting and passing? Play your own Cup Final at home with our table football game.

Kick off:
1 large grocery carton (approx. 60 x 35 cm)
2 soap powder packets
Thin dowelling or garden canes
22 spring-clip clothes pegs
Paint or sticky-backed plastic to cover box
Green and white stiff paper or paint
Gloss paint in colours of favourite teams
Stiff card for scoring discs and football figures
Numbers from old calendar
2 brass paper fasteners
Clear adhesive glue
Sticky tape
Table tennis ball to play game

First half:
Cut down a large grocery carton to make a shallow, open box with sides about 10 cm all round.

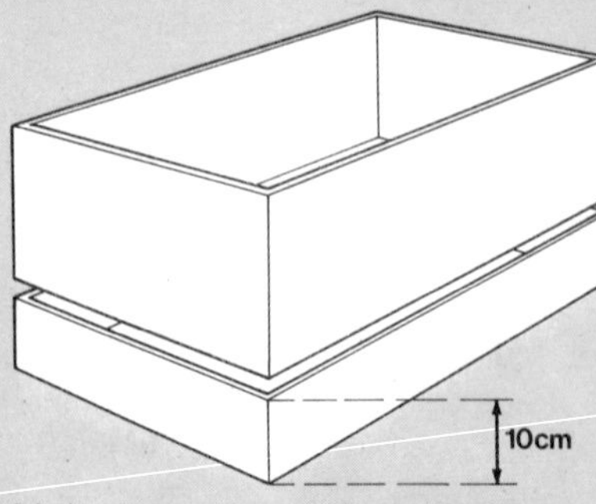

Make 2 goal boxes from the lower part of soap powder packets. For goal mouth cut away one long side as shown.

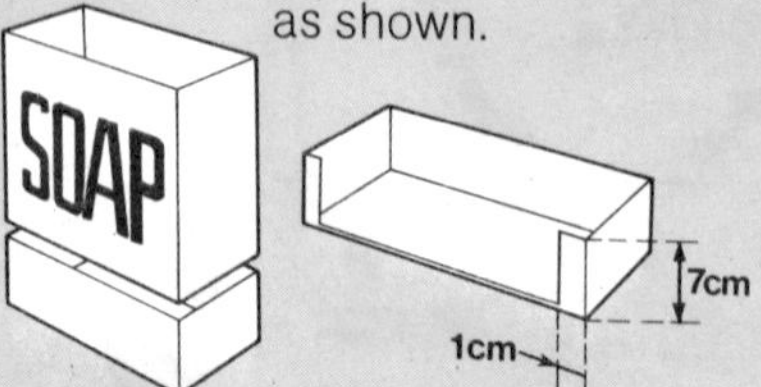

Place goal box against end of "field" making sure it's central, then draw round it. Remove the box and draw a second line 1 cm inside the first. Cut round this second line on three sides leaving a fold-down flap. Glue goal box onto flap and side of "field".

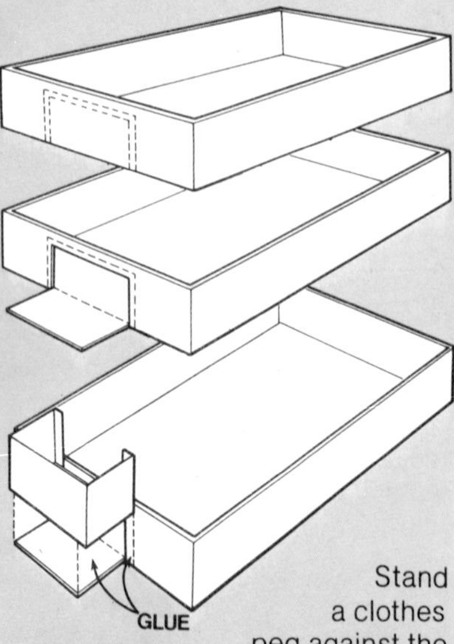

Stand a clothes peg against the side of "field" and mark the level of the peg hole. Make another mark 1 cm above. Do this at the other end of the box and draw a line joining the top marks together. Mark 8 evenly spaced holes along this line – make holes and test to see if they are large enough to take dowelling rods. Do this on both sides of the "field". The rods should turn easily.

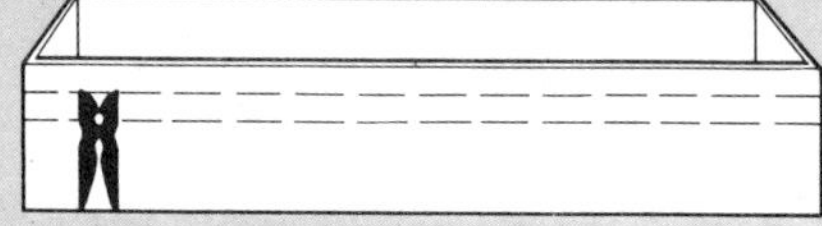

Use sticky tape to strengthen all the edges, then cover everything apart from the playing field with either paint or sticky-backed plastic.

Cut a thin frame from white card to outline the goalmouth and glue into place – or use white paint.

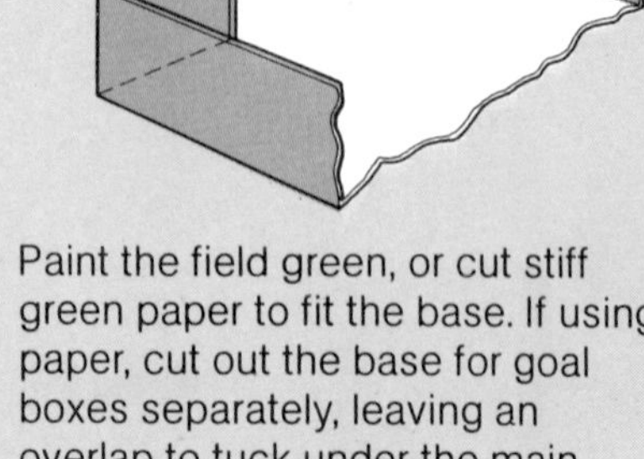

Paint the field green, or cut stiff green paper to fit the base. If using paper, cut out the base for goal boxes separately, leaving an overlap to tuck under the main sheet of paper. Glue these goal mouth pieces into place. Before glueing the main sheet mark the goal areas and centre line in white card or paint. Glue firmly in place.

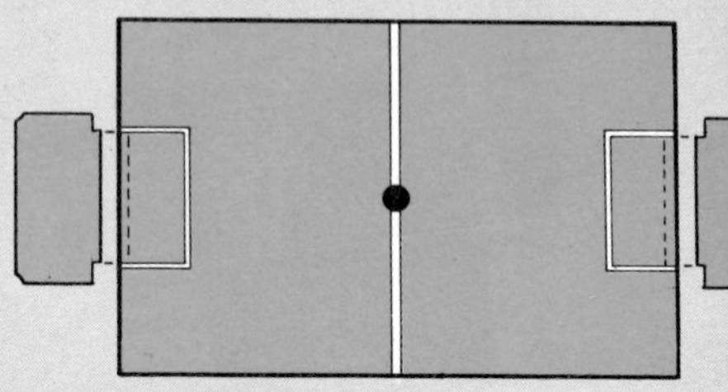

Half-time
If using paint, have a half-time rest and let it dry.

Second half:
To stop ball becoming stuck in the corners, cut four pieces of stiff green card about 7 cm square. Fold diagonally in half to make a triangle shape. Glue one in each corner.

Cut rods to size. They must be 25 cm longer than the width of the box. Smooth the ends with sand paper.

Cut out a pattern to make football figures, making sure it fits the size of pegs. Draw round pattern to make 44 figures from stiff card. Cut out and paint in your favourite team's colours. Glue the figures on each side of the 22 pegs.

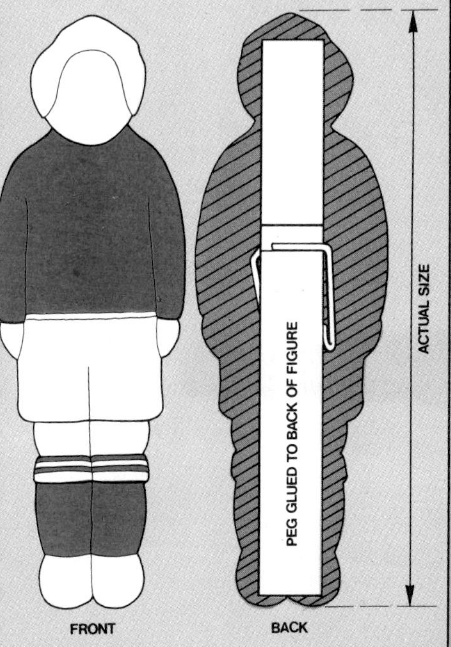

If you want a simpler version, you can just paint the pegs –10 in one colour and 10 in another, with 2 pegs painted green.

Slip the rods into place with equal amounts of rod on both sides of the box. Clip the pegs into place. (If any peg touches the ground, trim with sand paper.) When players are accurately in position, glue into place. Wind sticky tape round and round the ends of the rods to stop them pulling through the holes, and paint these ends to match the players on the rod.

Cut two scoring discs from stiff white card. Paint numbers – or cut out figures from an old calendar and glue round edge of disc. Attach to side of box with a brass paper fastener, positioning discs so that they overlap the corner of box to make turning easier.

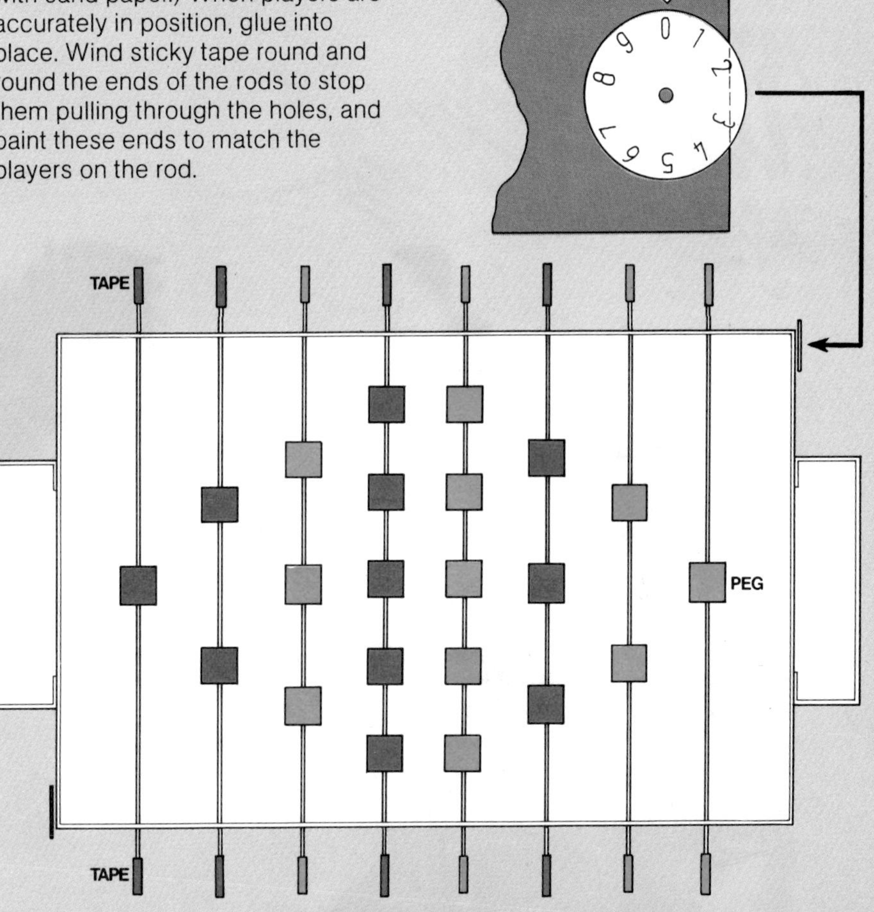

Full time:
Find another football fan. Toss a coin to see who throws the ball in and kick off! Get together a few of your friends, form your own league and have your own cup matches. Now you can have your own *Match of the Day* any time you like!

MYSTERY PICTURE

Colour the space as indicated by the numbers and the mystery picture will appear.

0 Leave white **1** Black **2** Light green **3** Dark green **4** Orange **5** Grey **6** Blue **7** Brown **8** Yellow **9** Pink **10** Red

XIII OLYMPIC WINTER GAMES LAKE PLACID 1980

WELCOME WORLD We're Ready!

"Can you ski, Tina?"

It was John Adcock, our Blue Peter Film Producer, on the telephone.

"Er – well, not very well," I said.

"How much have you done?"

"Well – none, actually."

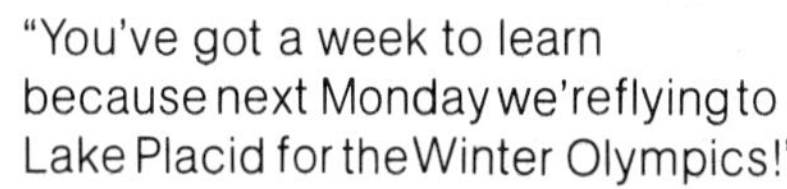

"You've got a week to learn because next Monday we're flying to Lake Placid for the Winter Olympics!"

The next morning I was at Hillingdon, 2800 miles from Lake Placid, but only 10 miles from my home. It was a lovely, sunny day, the temperature was in the 50s, and the countryside was green without a flake of snow in sight! But stretched out in front of me was the long, grey hill of the artificial ski-slope.

I was on skis, and Brian Martin was charged with teaching me to stand up in two rapid lessons.

"Lean forward, Tina – bend your knees – bend them further – keep your head up!"

It was never like this for Annmarie Moser, I thought, as I picked myself up for the hundredth time.

Two days later I checked in at London Airport for New York. I was on my way to Lake Placid.

"Welcome World – We're Ready!" read the huge slogan for the Winter Olympics.

They might be – but I'm not sure I am, I thought. Actually they weren't. The temperature was down to an unbelievable 30° below zero – too cold to think and nearly too cold to speak. But there was no snow – at least not nearly enough for the world's greatest skiers and ski jumpers to win Olympic titles on.

"What are you going to do?" I asked.

"Ma'am, if it doesn't snow, we'll just have to make it," said Craig, a tall, bearded American Olympic official. He pointed to huge pipes looking like the barrels of guns pointing into the air. Then he turned a switch, and gushing out of the barrels – unbelievably – came cascades of snow!

Craig told me that they just pump water and compressed air through the barrels – and at 30° below zero, Mother Nature did the rest.

"We've enough snow-making machines in Lake Placid to cover over ten miles of ski-runs to a depth of 40 cm in just sixteen hours!" said Craig, proudly.

All the snow on the towering ski-jumps was man-made. I'd never seen a ski-jump in real life, only on television, and the height was frightening. How anyone can launch themselves from the equivalent of Nelson's Column and land at the speed of an express train, I'll never know!

I did ski on the jump though – on the landing area! That's where I made my first attempt at a downhill run! My lessons at Hillingdon stood me in good stead, although the Lake Placid snow was much more slippery than Hillingdon's nylon carpet. But I managed to get down the slope – even if I didn't look like a world champion!

The Olympic flame that burns throughout the Games is lit in Greece, the home of the first Olympics. For the Winter Games, the flame was going to be flown from Greece to an American Air Force base in Virginia where fifty-two runners would carry it in relays to Lake Placid. The flame was just at the start of its journey when I reached Lake Placid, but I did try one of the special Olympic practice torches made to ensure the lighting of the flame in the Opening Ceremony would go off without a hitch. A special stadium had been built and from it you could get a view of every single event.

John set up the Blue Peter cameras to take the shot. Everything took double the length of time because the crew had to work in thick gloves most of the time because of the freezing temperatures. The cameraman looked down the lens – and the view disappeared! A blizzard had suddenly blown up out of the mountains,and we couldn't see farther than the seats in front of us.

I had already decided that Toni Innauer could rest happy in the knowledge that Tina Heath was not going to challenge him on the ski jump – so I went to watch the bobsledders, and that was worse! I remembered watching John Noakes crash on a bobsleigh in St Moritz, so I turned my attention to the lugers. They go down the run lying flat on their backs looking over their stomachs at the ice walls racing by – and I didn't fancy that either!

But I did skate on the Olympic ice. In two weeks' time, I thought as I looked up to rows of empty seats, Robin Cousins will be here going for a gold for Britain.

I gazed at the great electronic score board and prayed very hard for the boy from Bristol who'd come to the studio on Jack and Jill's birthday.

"Welcome World – We're Ready!" I thought – and *we* were!

e millions of visitors at Lake Placid could travel around on snowmobiles and take home their own tin of Winter Olympic snow.

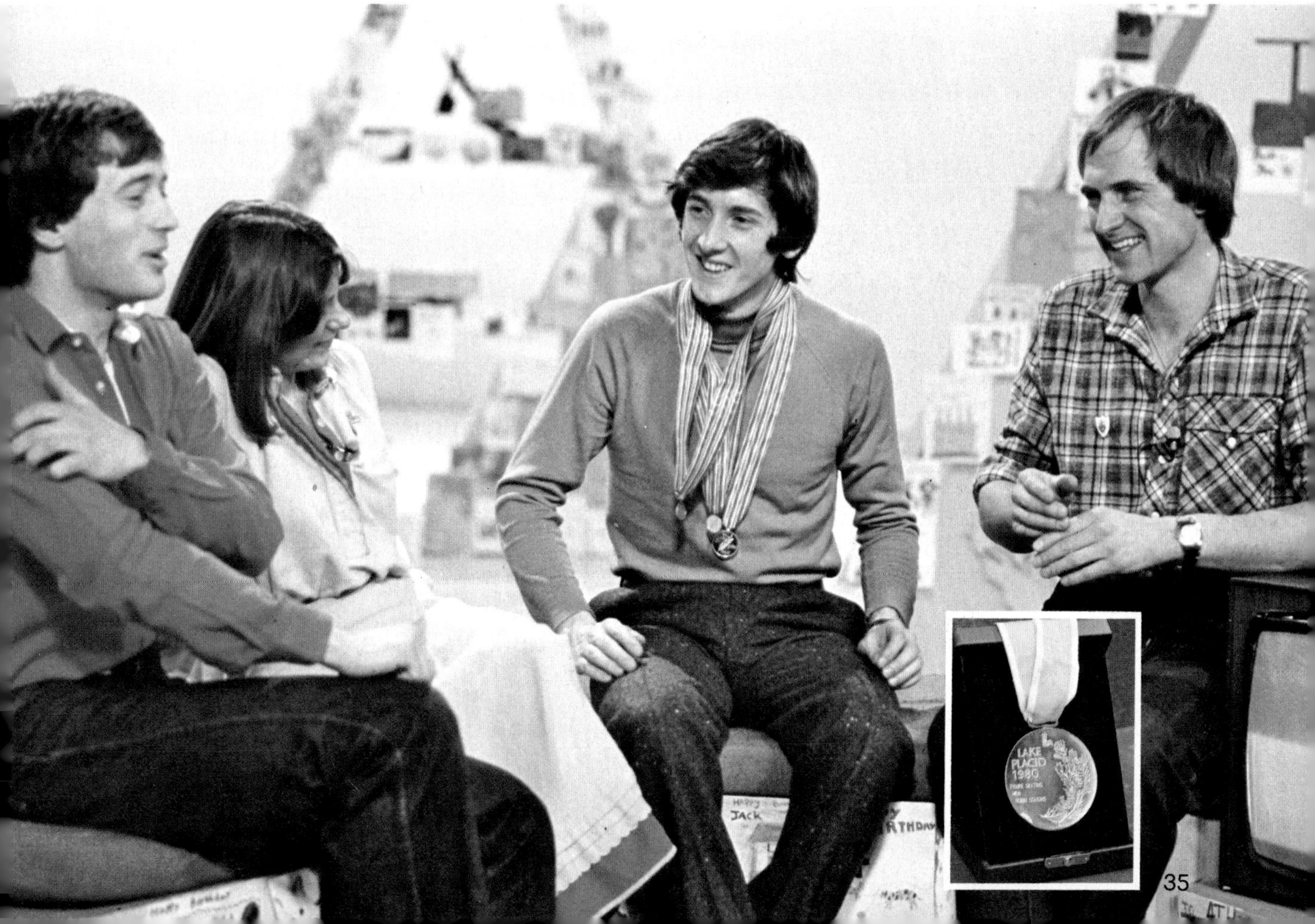

ABBEY NATIONAL!

Question: What's been called "The best-known and best-loved building in the English-speaking world"?

Answer: Westminster Abbey. Each year it's visited by more than 3½ million people, and millions more pass by outside. When I went to see it, I found it crammed full of strange and wonderful things. Walking through Westminster Abbey is like walking through history – these are just a few of the fascinating facts I discovered.

The most famous view of the Abbey, with the twin towers, was actually the last part to be finished, in 1745, seven hundred years after the Abbey was started. They were designed by Christopher Wren, who is much better known as the architect of St Paul's Cathedral, five miles away.

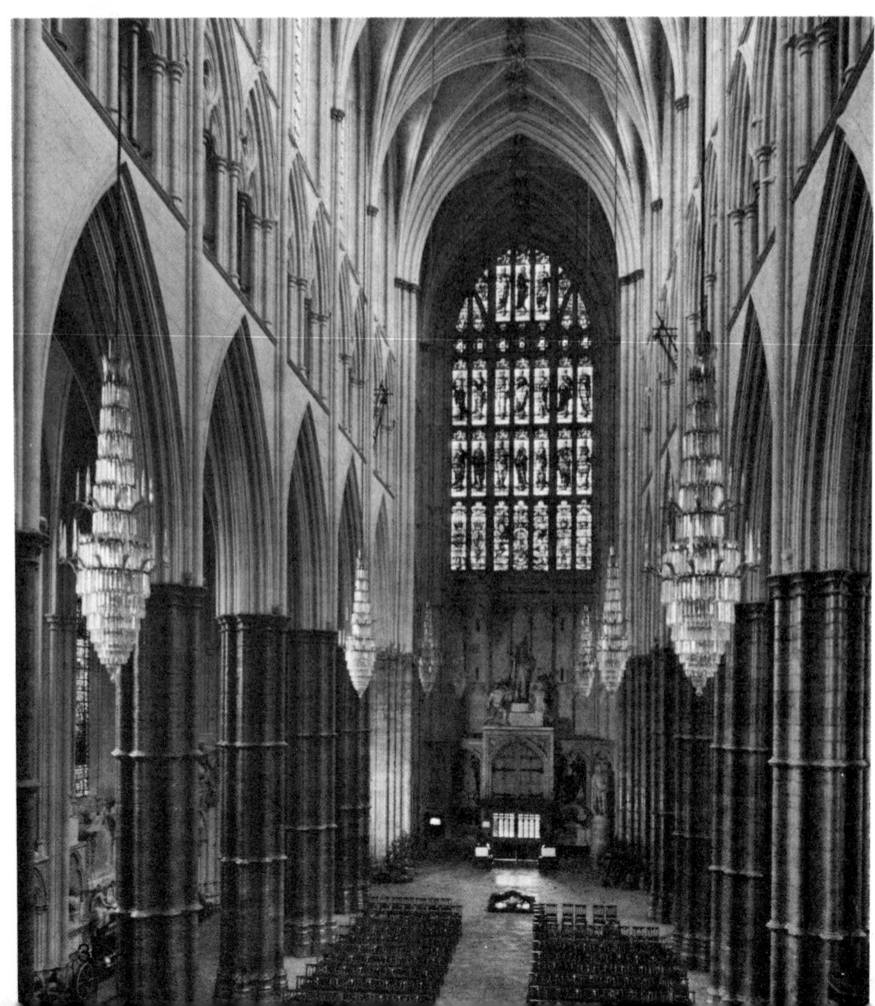

Not everything in the Abbey is old – though it has stood on the same spot for nearly a thousand years. This set of sparkling chandeliers was given fourteen years ago, as a 900th birthday present.

Inside the great West door, where everyone passes, is the tomb of the Unknown Warrior, surrounded by Flanders Poppies. It is there in honour of the millions who gave their lives in the 1914–18 war.

The High Altar, the heart of the Abbey, is raised on a mound of earth brought to Westminster all the way from the Holy Land.

Westminster Abbey was planned by King Edward the Confessor. It was finished in 1066, but later kings embarked on a new building, more glorious than anything Edward ever dreamt of. Edward was declared to be a saint, and he is buried in a splendid shrine designed by King Henry III. It was once decorated with rich jewels and gold statues.

England's greatest writers are remembered in Poets' Corner. I spotted memorials to Shakespeare, Kipling, Chaucer, the Brontë sisters, William Wordsworth and countless others.

In World War II, the Abbey's greatest treasures were packed up and carried to a London Underground station! They spent the war surrounded by sandbags, safe from the bombing.

Queen Elizabeth I is buried in the Abbey, and so is Mary Queen of Scots, her cousin, whom Elizabeth ordered to be beheaded.

Among all the kings and queens and mighty warriors lie two little girls, daughters of King James I. Princess Mary died when she was two.

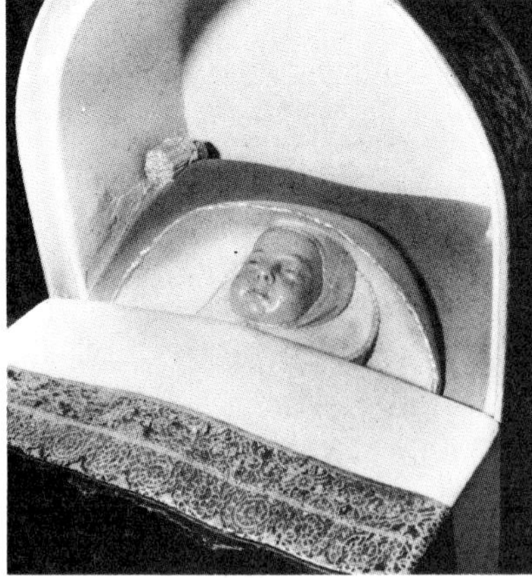

Princess Sophia only lived one day. She is called "a royal rosebud untimely picked by Death".

A coloured plaque in the cloisters celebrates the exploits of three men who never met each other at all. They were all master mariners who sailed round the world – Francis Drake in the sixteenth century, Captain James Cook in the eighteenth, and Francis Chichester only 13 years ago. I wonder if the men who explore the new worlds in space will be commemorated in the Abbey in years to come!

Edward the Confessor wanted his Abbey to be the Church where all the Kings and Queens of England were crowned. On Christmas Day, 1066, William the Conqueror was crowned here, and every British monarch since that day has held his or her coronation in Westminster Abbey.

The Coronation Chair contains a Stone which King Edward I captured and brought from Scotland. It is called the Stone of Destiny. In 1950, some Scots took it back to Scotland where they believed it truly belonged. It was away one hundred and four days until it appeared on the steps of a Scottish Abbey, and it was eventually restored to Westminster.

On 2 June 1953, Queen Elizabeth II was crowned in Westminster Abbey in the Coronation Chair, as all her ancestors had been before her.

THE GREAT BLUE PETE

In the middle of last October, a steady stream of letters reached the Blue Peter office – and they all said one thing. Could we possibly do <u>something</u> to help the horrific disaster that had happened in Cambodia?

One letter in particular stuck in our minds. It was sent to us by a Blue Peter viewer who was born in that part of South-East Asia, and who came to this country with his Thai mother and British father.

deAr Blue Peter,
LASt yeAr I came from Thailand.
NoW our neighbours The Kmers are Starving.
Would Blue Peter help oxfam noW.
AYe Davies.

The terrible facts were that not only had two million people died in Cambodia, but another <u>three</u> million were likely to starve to death by Christmas if help didn't reach them immediately.

It was probably the children who were suffering the most. A lot of them were very sick indeed after four years of malnutrition, and an eyewitness had reported that some were so poorly and weak that a puff of wind would blow them away!

John Craven gave us a special report on the Cambodia crisis.

One of the greatest problems was that the political situation in Cambodia was so complicated. John Craven, who had visited a Cambodian refugee camp for *Newsround* two years previously, came to our studio to explain what had been going on since 1975. John said because no one from the outside world had been allowed into Cambodia, all the dreadful horrors and tortures had happened in secret, and news was only just slowly trickling out.

The tragedy was that Cambodia used to be one of the most beautiful places in the world – lush and green with plenty of food for its seven million gentle people. But their happiness had come to an end in 1975 when a new and vicious government took over.

It was led by a man called Pol Pot, and his mad idea was for Cambodia to start all over again. He called 1975 Year Zero, and he set about his evil plan in the most appalling way. Pol Pot and his men, the Khmer Rouge, began to destroy everything that had been there before. Schools were banned, and so was music. Pol Pot didn't believe in families; so parents and children were split up. Everyone was ordered to toil in the fields. All there was in life was work and rest. And worst of all, Pol Pot set about killing at least one third of the people.

It's difficult to know what he and his

This little boy was dying from malnutrition.

men hoped to achieve by such cruelty. Pol Pot's destruction reduced the Cambodians to absolute poverty and despair. There was hardly any food to eat, and even less medicine, for as part of his plan to start from zero, Pol Pot killed nearly all of Cambodia's doctors and nurses. Even people wearing spectacles were murdered – because it proved they could read, and Pol Pot declared that "all past knowledge is illegal".

Pol Pot turned Phnom-Penh, the capital city, into a ghost town. He drove the people out to work as slaves in the countryside. He destroyed their Buddhist temples and churches of all other religions. He blew up the banks and the museums, and burned every single book in Phnom-Penh's library.

R BRING AND BUY SALE

In the countryside, things were even worse. Roads were destroyed and Pol Pot even closed the railway. And when he was eventually driven out, while the big nations of the world squabbled about who ruled Cambodia, little of the badly needed aid reached the desperate people.

By ignoring all the international politics, Oxfam was one of the few organisations that got on with the job of helping the starving, but much more help was needed to prevent millions of Cambodians dying before the end of the year.

We asked experts to advise us on exactly which basic supplies should be sent to Cambodia. Malcolm Harper, Oxfam's Communications Director, said the most important need was food. In one village, the rice ration was half a pound per person per month, and rice for the Cambodians is as basic as bread and potatoes are to us. The Cambodians needed to grow their own food, too – and wanted seeds like cabbage, soya, maize and rice, as well as rice to eat. To plant the seeds they needed hoes, because Pol Pot had destroyed even simple farming implements, and to give the starving people a chance to supplement their diet, they were desperate for fishing nets. Equally important, there was a need for lorries as these, too, had been destroyed by Pol Pot.

In the end we worked out that one lorry plus 70 tons of rice, 42 tons of seeds, 10,000 hoes and 1000 fishing nets would cost no less than one hundred thousand pounds!

It was a colossal task, but the emergency was so terrible, we felt we had to try. But there was no time to ask Blue Peter viewers to collect scrap commodities as we usually do. The reclamation of the rubbish would take far too long and we needed the £100,000 – fast!

Phnom-Penh – once one of the most beautiful capital cities in the world – was destroyed by Pol Pot and his vicious government. This mother and baby were driven from their home by heartless Khmer Rouge troops.

We all racked our brains to think of a solution and it was our boss, Edward Barnes, the Head of BBC Children's Programmes, who came up with what turned out to be a life-saving idea.

Oxfam's 584 shops all held sales.

"Why not use all the Oxfam shops for a Great Blue Peter Bring and Buy Sale?" he suggested – and that's how the biggest Bring and Buy Sale in the world began! To be fair to all the viewers who didn't live near one of the Sale shops, we suggested that they held their own do-it-yourself Great Blue Peter Bring and Buy Sales – and to our amazement, the idea snowballed. The Blue Peter office became like a telephone exchange as viewers phoned in to check where they could get their posters, price tags and Blue Peter Cambodia stickers.Our British Isles map fairly bristled with red and yellow dots as gradually the "do-it-yourself" sales overtook the Oxfam shops and we ended up with more than 12,000 Great Blue Peter Bring and Buy Sales, and with over 12 million Blue Peter Cambodia stickers distributed to the Bringers and Buyers.

We visited shops in England, Northern Ireland, Scotland and Wales.

The sales hit the headlines in all the national and provincial papers. We were asked to broadcast on local radio stations and Radios 1, 2 and 4. John Craven's *Newsround* filmed in the Blue Peter office, and so did Prakesh Mirchandani for the BBC's main news bulletins.

Looking back it seems quite natural that what turned out to be the world's biggest Bring and Buy Sale should produce such phenomenal results. But it's still hard to believe what happened! To our complete and utter amazement, we reached our £100,000 Target in two days.

Jim Grant, our designer, who'd created our Totaliser to flash up the figures, thought we were pulling his leg as we phoned through to order more and more noughts. It was a staggering moment when we rang to say: "We've reached a million pounds, Jim!"
Little did we think then that we'd end up with nearly four times that amount.

The sad thing was that the Bring and Buy Sale proceeds that seemed such a huge amount to us were just a drop in the ocean of what was needed. This was why we kept raising our Targets. Malcolm Harper, who was reporting back to us from Phnom-Penh, sent heartbreaking descriptions of the devastation.

Journalist John Pilger, who gave us an eyewitness account of Cambodia's suffering.

Journalist John Pilger, who'd been one of the first foreigners allowed into Phnom-Penh after Pol Pot and his men had been driven out, told us how much the children were suffering. He said it would be months before the dangers of starvation were over, and years before Cambodia was back to normal.

HITTING THE HEADLINES!

Suddenly the Great Blue Peter Bring & Buy Sale was hot news.

Cameras from Newsround and the main bulletins filmed in the Blue Peter office as your donations passed the £1,000,000 mar

Do-it-yourself Great Blue Peter Bring & Bu Sales mushroomed all over Britain.

OUR GREAT BLUE PETER BRING & BUY SALE AUCTION!

Some of the Cambodian bank notes I'd found lying in the gutter in Phnom-Penh.

DO-IT-YOURSELF GREAT BLUE PETER BRING & BUY SALES AND STUNTS!

Home-made bookmarks, Christmas cards and gift tags, and even mouth-watering Blue Peter cookies all helped to save the lives of starving Cambodian babies and children.

Heddwyn Taylor of mid-Glamorgan grew half a beard and raised over £2,000.

Two of the many vehicles viewers gave us to boost our funds.

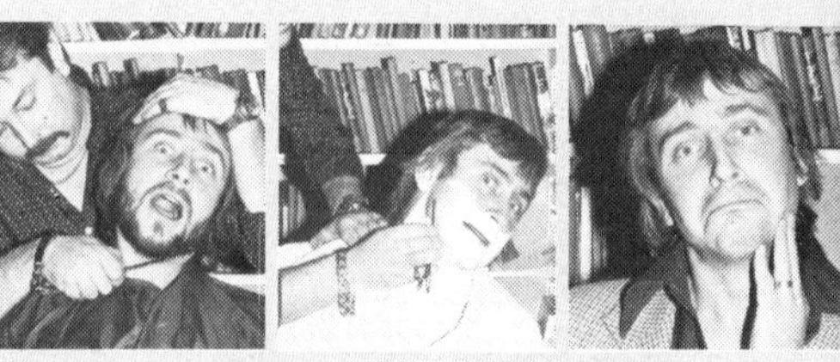

Radio Nottingham's John Holmes shaved off his beard in his local Oxfam shop to publicise the Appeal.

Altogether, over 12,000 Do-it-yourself Bring & Buy Sales were held.

A precious Victorian locket was auctioned by Radio Humberside. And Radio Leicester's 3-day auction raised £6766.

Lot No. 101 was a very special one for me – I bought these two rings for my wedding in September.

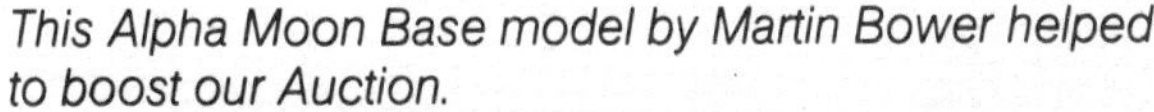

This Alpha Moon Base model by Martin Bower helped to boost our Auction.

Our biggest Lot! A giant panda made by the 2nd Hornchurch Girls' Brigade. Altogether, our Auction raised £10,789.50p.

THE CAMBODIANS
who gave us first-hand accounts of the dreadful plight of families and friends they'd left behind.

We talked to lots of Cambodian eyewitnesses, too. A doctor who'd escaped before Pol Pot took over had just heard that one of his sisters and her husband had survived. His brother-in-law, a University lecturer, pretended to be a rag-and-bone man to escape being murdered. His sister's baby had been born on the side of the road, as they were driven out of Phnom-Penh, and she and her husband were sent to a forced labour camp to clear forests with their bare hands. His brother-in-law had a huge hump of skin on his shoulder after months of being used as a human truck for carrying heavy tree trunks.

Nearly every relation of this doctor was murdered.

Var Hong and her children, Somaly and Panita, who escaped from forced labour camps.

Var Hong, who'd been a primary school teacher in Phnom-Penh, told us how she and her two little girls, Somaly – then aged 8 – and Panita – aged 4 – had also been put in a

Hak Srea demonstrated one of the Khmer typewriters provided by our Appeal.

labour camp. The Khmer Rouge tried to trick Var Hong into revealing she could read and write. She and the children were given thin rice gruel as their only food and Var and Somaly were forced to work clearing a forest. Even four–year-old Panita had to work 18 hours a day collecting dung to be used as fertiliser. One day the camp leaders ordered Var to bicycle to another camp with a message. She was so weak she fell off, breaking her collar-bone. Because she was given no medical treatment, Var's collar bone will always be twisted, and she also has the scars of anthrax on her wrist and arm – a disease that only animals get in Europe, but one that many Cambodians were infected by because of their severe malnutrition and lack of medical care.

Out of 500 people in Var's camp, only three survived. She and the children managed to make their way to the north-west where they escaped across the Thailand border and where missionaries brought them to England. But although they survived, not one of their many relations is known to be alive.

It's difficult for anyone living in Britain or anywhere in the Western world to begin to understand what the Cambodians suffered. Even the poorest person in the West is like a millionaire compared with people who have been starved and tortured and deprived not only of their homes and all their possessions, but of the basic necessities of life that we all take for granted.

OUR SUPPLIES GET THROUGH!
On 26th, November 1979, Simon became the first British Reporter allowed into Phnom-Penh since John Pilger left in August.

On 26th November, I became the first British reporter allowed into Phnom-Penh since John Pilger left in August. The experience will haunt me for the rest of my life. The whole city looked as though it had been struck by a tornado or an earthquake. But the devastated buildings, the streets piled high with rubble, the baths, refrigerators, washing machines and cookers rotting on the sides of the roads, the ruined hospitals, temples, banks and libraries, were all destroyed deliberately. I picked up handfuls of bank notes from the gutter – all quite useless as Pol Pot had declared money illegal, and now the country was so devastated, there was nothing money could buy.

How *could* Cambodians ever pick up the threads of normal life? Only with massive help from the outside world. A great deal of the aid was being held up because of political arguments, but some *was* trickling through and I had living proof of that as I'd flown into Phnom-Penh with some of our own Blue Peter lorries and the other supplies provided by the Great Blue Peter Bring and Buy Sale. I visited an orphanage with Malcolm and saw how lucky the children were who *had* been getting more food as the rice was distributed, and how our hoes were being used to cultivate the land for the next harvest.
Malcolm told me how small factories were being set up to make fishing nets from the twine we were supplying, and plastic utensils for homes and hospitals. Slowly, very slowly, the recovery was starting.
If the supplies are kept up, and *if* the nations of the world allow the Cambodians to run their country for themselves, the chances are Cambodia will survive.

Thanks to the massive help *you* gave, thousands of babies and children and adults have been saved from death. The Great Blue Peter Bring and Buy Sale was a record breaker, but we all hope there'll never ever be another tragedy that requires such desperate measures.

This little girl clung to me in the orphanage I visited. Her parents had been murdered.

Rice and rice seed about to be distributed.

Our hoes helping to provide the next harvest.

Malcolm Harper, Oxfam's Communications Director, who was in charge of the distribution of all the Great Blue Peter Bring & Buy Sale supplies. I flew in to Phnom-Penh with some of our lorries.

We will continue to accept all donations for Cambodia. By 28 May, 1980, the Great Blue Peter Bring and Buy Sale had reached £3,689,046, which had supplied:

57 eight-ton lorries to deliver vital supplies (including 2 lorries plus a breakdown/repair lorry donated by British Leyland's Bathgate factory)
27,000 gallons of diesel fuel
2300 tons of rice
5500 tons of rice seed
310,000 hoes to help plant seed

The hire of a DC10 aircraft for 18 days to airlift seed to Phnom-Penh.

One ferry to take supplies across the Mekong River.

3000 tons of fertilisers
1000 fishing nets
10 tons of fishing net twine
1000 doses of vaccine
82 tons of cotton yarn to weave into cloth for clothes
200 irrigation pumps
30 tons of raw plastic for hospital and household utensils
10 typewriters with Khmer type face

Out of this colossal amount of aid, only just over one per cent of your donations has been spent on administrative costs!

CHRISTMAS GARLANDS

Here's an idea for something you can make in a jiffy if you're short of a decoration or two at Christmas. As well as being quick and easy, it's a real money saver, and although you *can* use coloured paper, a white garland looks very snowy and winterish.

For one garland, all you need is: A few bits of tinsel and ribbon, a piece of kitchen foil, a bit of stiff garden wire (or a *thin* wire coat hanger) and three sheets of tissue paper. Bend the wire into a circle to make the frame.

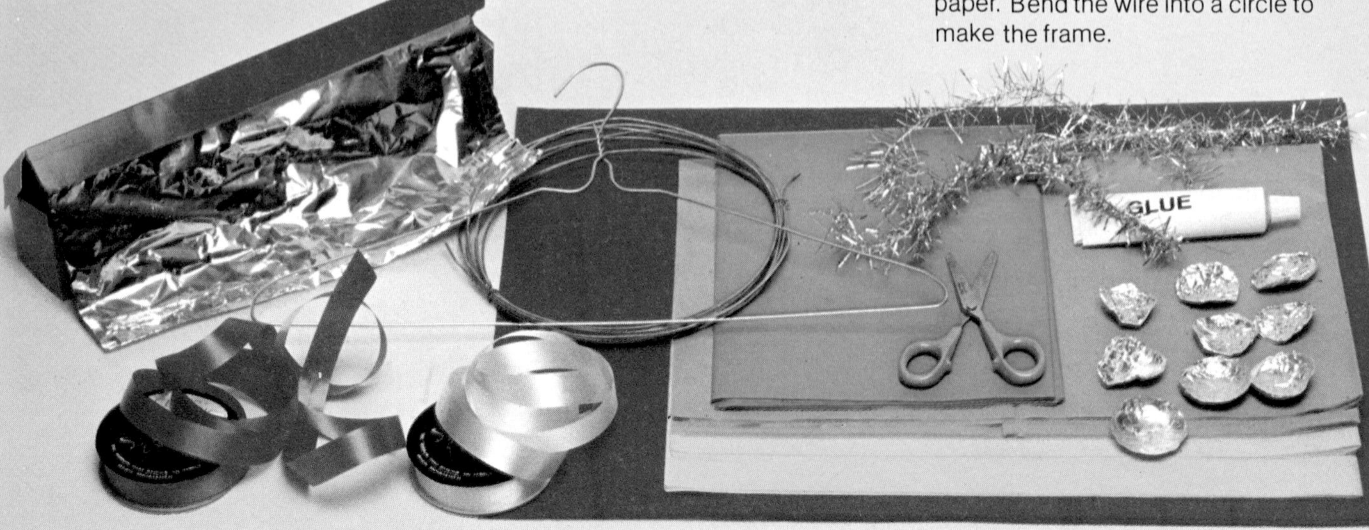

Leaves

1 Mark one sheet of the tissue paper in squares of about 10 cm. Put the other two sheets underneath and cut out all three sheets at once.

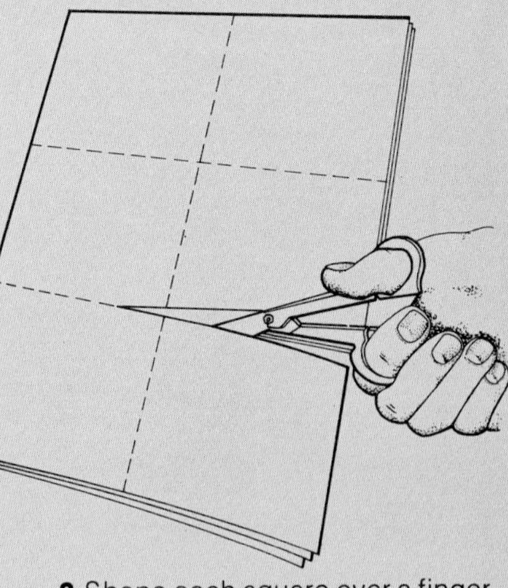

2 Shape each square over a finger, pulling the paper round the finger with your other hand.

3 Push the wire through the flattened end of each leaf – about 1 cm from the end – and thread all the leaves on to the frame. (Stick a cork or a piece of sticky tape on one end of the wire to stop them falling off.)

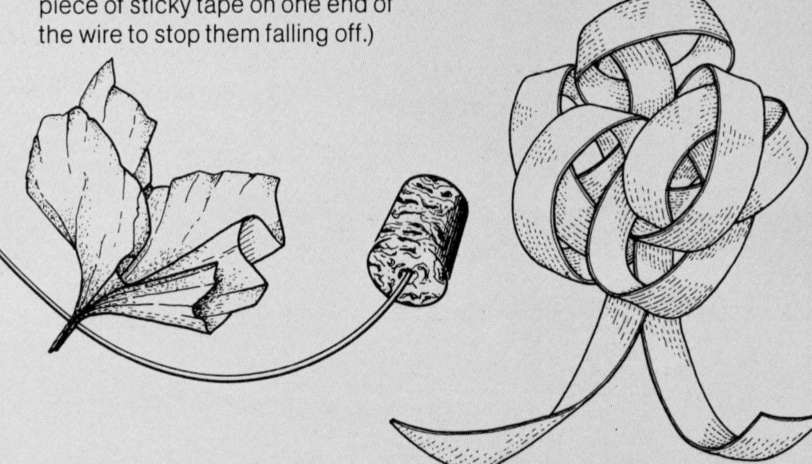

4 Add the leaves until the frame is thickly covered, leaving just a short piece of wire at each end. You'll get a nice rounded shape if you alternate the points of the leaves so that one points inwards and the next outwards etc. as you push them on.

5 When the frame's full, push the last few leaves on either side down and bind the ends of the wire together with sticky tape. Make a hook from a short piece of wire and tape it on securely, making sure it's a big one, otherwise the garland won't hang properly.

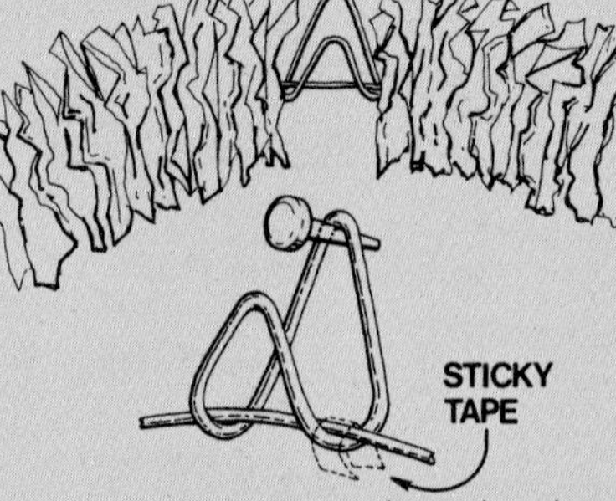

6 Ease the leaves back again, close to the sticky tape, and hide the hook with a large bow from gift ribbon held on with tape or fuse wire. (If you're no good at big bows, make three or four small ones with long ends and fasten them together.)

Flowers

7 Make seven of these, using 7 circles of kitchen foil shaped over your finger like the leaves. Complete the centre of each flower with a dab of glue and a piece of tinsel.

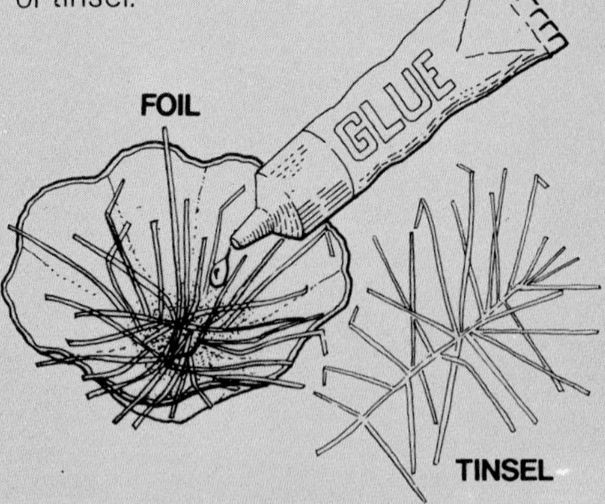

Glue the flower onto the garland. If you've run out of kitchen foil, milk bottle tops are just as good, but you'll need more, as they're small. For a finishing touch, glue tiny scraps of tinsel in the spaces *between* the flowers and get an extra Christmas sparkle!

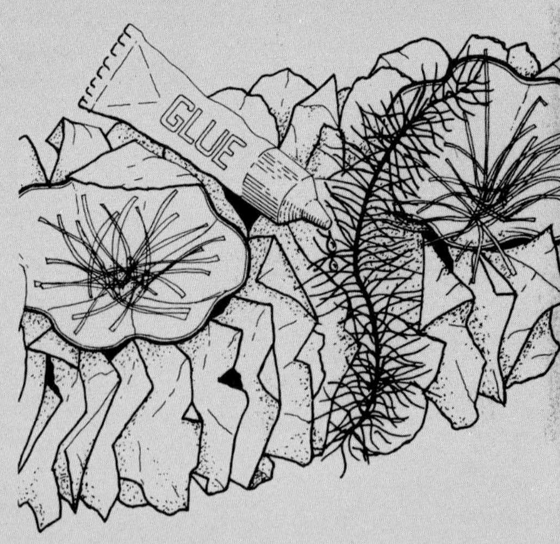

"The Seven Wonders of the Ancient World" sound like something out of a fairy tale. We were lucky enough to see one of them during our Expedition to Egypt – the pyramids.

EG

I always thought the pyramids were smooth. It's only when you get close that you realise they're made up of huge blocks of limestone, piled tier upon tier.

The biggest of the three pyramids, at Giza near Cairo, was built as a burial place for King Cheops, the Pharaoh who ruled Egypt 4500 years ago. The ancient Egyptians believed in life after death, so when their Pharaoh died, furniture, food and treasures were buried with him for his journey into the next world.

Three million blocks of stone were used in the pyramid of Cheops alone – some weighing 30 tons each. Originally it stood 146 metres tall, but the peak has been worn away by time, and now it's a mere 134 metres. A French mathematician once worked out that there was enough stone in the three pyramids at Giza to build a wall 30cm thick and 3 metres high right round the whole of France!

It was an eerie feeling standing where Caesar and Antony and Cleopatra had also stood and gazed in awe at the pyramids nearly 2000 years ago. Today they are empty – their untold riches plundered by robbers over the centuries. All that remains in the pyramid of Cheops is the granite coffin or sarcophagus where the king's body was laid to rest. This is in a chamber in the heart of the pyramid, and one of the most extraordinary things about it is that it's fully air-conditioned! Just above the floor are shafts that let in fresh air. Some say this was to preserve the body – but others say it was to let the Pharaoh's spirit out.

Lying at the foot of the three

I climbed the first twenty tiers of the pyramids. Egyptians are trying to stop tourists climbing to the very top because of the damage they are doing to the stones. It's dangerous, too! I was quite glad not to have to climb all the way up – at ten o'clock in the morning, the temperature was nearing 100 degrees F!

YPT

pyramids is a beast as famous as the pyramids themselves. The Sphinx, with the body of a lion and the face of a man, has a mysterious smile that has fascinated people for centuries.

We couldn't leave Giza without seeing the pyramids at sunset, and what better way than from the back of a camel. We found a man called Abdul who certainly took us for a ride! He hired us three camels at vast expense to make the trip. "My camels are film stars, Mister," he told us. "They were in *Death on the Nile*." My camel had a film star's name, too. He was called Mickey Mouse, and we were getting on fine until halfway through our trip when his saddle became loose, and I joined the long line of Blue Peter Presenters who've bitten the sands of the desert, thrown from the back of a bad-tempered camel!

I climbed 27 metres up into the middle of the pyramid to the burial chamber itself. It was quite an eerie climb. The main staircase is inside a vast 30-metre-high corridor, and the walls are limestone blocks locked together so tightly that even today you can't insert a needle between the stones.

I discovered another burial place. This hole in the ground wasn't for a man, but for a boat. The Egyptians believed their Pharaohs would need boats in the next world to sail across the sky. It was discovered in 1954. Now the boat has been removed and a museum built round it to preserve it for future generations.

Luxor

The secret city of Karnak lies on the East bank of the River Nile at Luxor. Simon and I were overwhelmed by this city of temples, dedicated to Ammon, the greatest god of Ancient Egypt. For two thousand years the Pharaohs kept adding to the city. And as each one wanted *his* temple to be the best, the buildings grew more and more impressive.

Only priests and the Pharaohs were allowed to enter Karnak. Some of the giant buildings had secret staircases inside the walls which were believed to be the stairs to heaven. In 1903 a grave was opened up revealing thousands of statues piled one on top of the other. There were 800 stone and 17,000 bronze statues – and you can see some of them today in the British Museum.

Pharaoh Rameses II finished the most amazing part of Karnak – the Hall of Columns! This vast hall has 134 columns. Most of them are 15 metres high, but the centre 12 columns tower nearly 23 metres and they are so wide it's said that a hundred people could stand on the top of each one!

A fallen giant – Rameses II lying on his back, a victim of ancient vandalism.

Rameses II thought big. There are giant statues of him all over Egypt. The biggest is in his funeral temple, built to keep his memory alive after his death. It's now in several pieces, knocked down, historians believe, by Persian invaders, two and a half thousand years ago. But what a monster it must have been! It was carved out of a solid piece of granite weighing over 1000 tons and would have stood over 23 metres high. The Pharoah's fingers alone are a metre long.

Rameses's temple stands on the west bank of the Nile, near the Valley of the Kings – a hiding place where Pharaohs were buried. One by one, the tombs were discovered and plundered, but for 3300 years, one tomb kept its secrets. Then, in November 1922, Howard Carter, an English archaeologist, made one of the most exciting discoveries ever – he found the tomb of Tutankhamun. After months of digging, they reached the doorway

to the tomb. Carter stood, riveted.

"What can you see?" clamoured the men behind him.

At first, Carter was speechless – then still gazing at his discoveries, he breathed: "Wonderful things!"

In six years, over two thousand objects were found including the most famous of all – Tutankhamun's solid gold death mask. But not everything was taken from the tomb. In respect for the dead king, the Egyptians left his body in its gold-plated casket lying in the sarcophagus. Tutankhamun was only 18 years old when he died, and was probably an unimportant Pharaoh, but because of the amazing treasure found by Howard Carter, he has become the most famous of them all.

Red Sea

The Red Sea is oddly named, as it's the bluest sea I've ever seen. The waters are crystal clear, making it a paradise for underwater swimmers. Simon and Tina had never done snorkelling before. I did quite a bit when I lived in El Salvador, but the underwater scenery off the coast at Hurghada was more beautiful than anything I had seen. Captain Achmed, an expert Egyptian diver, warned us: "Don't touch the coral because it's as sharp as a razor and don't touch any fish because a lot of them are poisonous. As a general rule, the more beautiful the fish, the more dangerous they are!"

I took along a home movie camera to try my hand at underwater photography and the results weren't too bad. They make a marvellous record of our underwater exploration of the Red Sea.

This is the 8mm film I shot

Obelisks

There is a quarry at Aswan where the ancient Egyptians carved obelisks. These huge fingers of stone covered with mysterious hieroglyphic writing which have found their way to many of the capitals of the world – like London's Cleopatra's Needle – all come from this one quarry.

No one knows exactly how the huge obelisks – hewn from solid granite – were transported 3,500 years ago, but a clue does exist as to how they were quarried – and we walked along it! It was an unfinished obelisk still attached to the bed-rock. It was abandoned because cracks appeared after the work had started.

Although most people have heard of Cleopatra, there was another Queen of Egypt who left her mark in a big way. Queen Hatchepsut holds the record for the tallest obelisk. It stands over 30 metres high, and was part of her temple at Karnak.

Aswan

Egypt holds the Blue Peter record for the hottest place we've ever explored. It was an unbelievable 140 degrees F. in the shade, and we found the best place to cool off was the Aswan High Dam. The thundering power of the water shoots out, filling the air with a fine spray that wraps around you like a constant cold shower.

Before the dam was built, the River Nile used to dry up in the hot summer, and often the crops failed. But since 1971, the High Dam has provided farmers with all the water they need, although building it brought its own problems. Many ancient Egyptian temples would have disappeared under the rising waters of the Nile if something hadn't been done to save them.

I saw the results of two incredible rescue operations. The temples at Philae and Abu Simbel were both moved stone by stone to higher ground. The whole operation was a race against time. It was a colossal task that cost millions of pounds because the archaeologists insisted that the buildings must be reconstructed exactly as they were. At Philae no stone is more than two millimetres out of its original position.

Today the temples look as though they have stood on their new sites for thousands of years. But without the Egyptians' brilliant reconstruction, they would have disappeared beneath the waters of the Nile for ever!

ECCLESIASTICAL KNOCKERS

One of these giant door knockers is nearly 900 years old – the other was made in 1979! Can you tell which is which?

Durham Cathedral is one of Britain's top tourist attractions. Towering massively above the banks of the River Wear, it's more like a castle than a cathedral, and visitors from all over the world know it as England's finest example of early Norman architecture. But one of the cathedral's greatest treasures is not a piece of stained glass or an ancient statue, it's a door knocker – a massive bronze face that's been a familiar sight on the north door for the last 825 years.

It's a "Sanctuary" knocker, which means that in the olden days, criminals fleeing from justice who made their way to the cathedral could cling to its stout bronze ring and claim refuge or sanctuary.

Once inside the cathedral, no criminal could be punished, but they had to confess to what they had done, and swear that they would leave the country for ever. They had to wear a black gown with a yellow cross of St Cuthbert on the left shoulder and were sent to a port to take the very first ship leaving England.

Now visitors to the Cathedral can see the new knocker on the North Door and the original in the Treasury.

In 1977 the knocker was discovered to be in need of repair. It was removed from the North Door, and because of its great age and rarity, it was sent to no less than the British Museum for expert attention.

In January 1980, we gave the restored knocker its first-ever public showing, and also announced the rather sad news that it could never be put back outside on the North Door as experts at the Museum felt that atmospheric pollution would cause even greater damage.

Fortunately, the Dean and Chapter came up with an excellent idea. They asked Metal Sculptor Michael Gillespie to make a replica, and when we saw it next to the knocker, all of us in the studio found it practically impossible to tell the two apart.

Now Durham Cathedral has two Sanctuary knockers. The replica is fixed in place on the North Door – its weird and rather spooky face staring at all the passers-by. But the original is still on view. It has pride of place in the Cathedral Treasury, where it's hung on a wooden panel so that visitors can still touch it – just like the men and women fleeing from justice all those hundreds of years ago.

Meanwhile, ba

When I go abroad on a Blue Peter filming trip, there's only one sadness. I can't take Goldie with me. The quarantine regulations which keep rabies out of Britain, mean that I would have to put her in kennels for six months as soon as we got back to London Airport! But for Goldie, it's not that bad, because she goes off to my Dad's farm in Dethick where she enjoys a reunion with all her old friends.

Goldie's training really has paid off. She can be trusted with all the animals on the farm.

Emma, the goat, looks as though she's about to charge . . . but she's really quite friendly.

This is Gem, the Collie who helps my Dad on the farm.

k on the farm...

My Mum's one of Goldie's biggest fans.

Tea time for Oscar – and Goldie waits hopefully for the leftovers!

HERE WE ARE AGAIN!

The Story of Joey the Clown

All over the world, clowns are known as Joey. They are called after one man who was born in London more than two hundred years ago, on 18 December 1779. His name was Joseph Grimaldi.

1 Joe Grimaldi made his first appearance as an imp at Sadler's Wells Theatre when he was only two years old. His mother was a young dancer, his father an Italian settled in England, who was 65 when Joe was born.

2 Old Grim, as he was called, was determined to make his son work in the theatre. One day he dressed Joe in a "skin" as a monkey and swung him round and round on the end of a chain. The chain broke, and Joe fell into the lap of a surprised elderly man in the audience.

3 At five years old, Joe played the Cat in the pantomime at Drury Lane, but he tripped over his tail and fell down a trap door. He broke his collar bone and it was the end of pantomime for him for that season. All his life, disasters and the applause of the audience went together.

4 Old Grim was a gloomy man. In their time off he took his son for walks in London graveyards. It was a strange life for a future clown – but Joe never felt tragedy and comedy were far apart.

5 When he was nine, his father died and Joe had to earn his living in earnest. He was too old to play imps and not old enough for grown-up parts. He spent all his time learning about the theatre.

6 He experimented with make-up, and painted his face in strange ways. He always saw himself as a clown – a comic actor – and never wanted to go into serious drama. As he grew older, he got better parts.

7 When he was 22, he had a great chance. He partnered a star actor who played Gobble, the Eating Clown. At last he was a clown at Drury Lane, and a huge success. Joe was at the top of the comic world.

8 But when he was not on the stage making people laugh, Joe was often sad and lonely. He took up pigeon fancying and spent quiet hours alone in his pigeon loft.

9 He had another accident on stage – a pistol misfired and he was badly burnt. He finished the performance in great pain, but a dancer called Mary Bristow was very kind to him.

10 Joe married her and they had a son, called Joseph Samuel. They hoped he would be a star one day, but Joe was determined the boy should not have the hard childhood *he* had known.

11 At Christmas in 1806, when he was twenty-seven, Joe Grimaldi scored his greatest triumph. He starred in a new pantomime, called Mother Goose, or The Golden Egg. The audience loved it, and it has been a firm favourite ever since. Grimaldi, Joey the Clown, was hailed as the funniest man in London. Everyone knew him, and his catch phrase – "Here we are again!" He was popular with rich and poor, old and young, high and low brow. One night King George III was there, in a very tight General's uniform. It was said "he laughed almost to suffocation at Grimaldi's exhibition of swallowing a quantity of long puddings."

12 All the theatres wanted Joe. Sometimes he would play at Sadler's Wells and then run three miles through the streets to appear at Covent Garden, wearing his clown's costume, with a great crowd following him.

13 One night there was a party of sailors in the gallery, including a man deaf and dumb after a bad attack of sunstroke. Suddenly this man turned to his mates, saying: "What a funny fellow!" "Why, Jack, can you speak?" they exclaimed. "Aye, and hear, too!" the sailor said cheerfully. The tale of how Joey the Clown cured a deaf and dumb sailor spread all over London.

14 For twenty years Grimaldi was supreme in the theatre, but he was not the same off-stage. He was a quiet, friendly man, worried about his son who had turned out badly, and in great pain from arthritis, caused by all his accidents and hard work.

15 At last, when he was only 49, he gave his farewell performance. "I'll play tonight if it costs me my life," Joe declared. The theatre was crammed full – the audience he had made laugh so often, were in tears that night.

The Clowns Service

Now every year, clowns from all over Britain gather together at Holy Trinity Church, Dalston, for a service in Joe Grimaldi's honour, and to lay a wreath on his memorial.

This year was the 34th Annual Clowns' service and the sermon was preached by the Bishop of Stepney.

When one of the clowns laid the wreath, the Chaplain said: "We remember the life of your servant, known as Grimaldi the Clown; his skill and artistry, and the pleasure he brought to many. Surely he helped you to touch some of your children's hearts by the droll gaiety of his acting, and for this we give thanks. Amen."

In the grease paint tracks of Grimaldi

No it isn't Kojak, it's me being transformed by Jo Young of the BBC Make Up Department into Joe Grimaldi.

This is the original clown make up, invented by Grimaldi on which every clown's face has been based from that day to this.

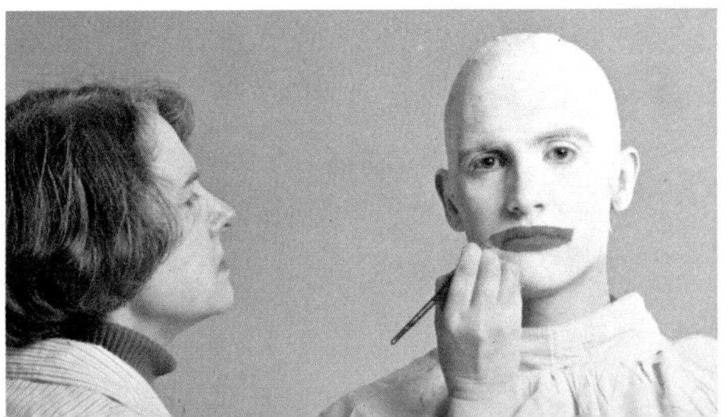

THE CASE OF **THE LION OF VENICE**

Can you solve this case? Six careless mistakes gave away the crooks.

We spotted them – can you?

The gondola turned once more into the breathtaking Grand Canal of Venice and Bob said: "I don't think I'll ever get over this place."

His uncle, a private detective of international fame, ex-Police-Superintendent McCann, laughed. "It always gets you the first time. But don't think the people of Venice ride around in gondolas like this. They're strictly for the tourists like us."

Bob grinned. "How are you enjoying being a tourist instead of a detective for a change?"

"I've just been working on a really tricky case in the Middle East – it's good to take a few days holiday for once."

Bob said: "Well, it's certainly great for me to take a break after a hard term at college. It's good to be here. Venice is unbelievable. Why did they build all these canals instead of normal streets?"

"The first Venetians were fleeing from their enemies, and they ran to the middle of this lagoon for safety," explained McCann. "They built up islands for their city – but here we are back at our hotel."

Bob looked towards the water gate of their hotel and started. A dapper, suited figure with his tie awry and a contorted expression on his face was waving to them, and there was desperation in his wave. "Do you know him?" Bob asked.

"Never seen him in my life," muttered McCann as the gondola drew to a halt.

The dark Italian took a step forward and half-helped, half-pulled McCann ashore in his eagerness to speak to the great detective: "Thanka the Lord you are in Venice, Signor McCann. For my city, she has been a-robbed of a great treasure. You musta help me!"

"Hmm," said McCann. "So much for being a tourist." They walked into the hotel with Bob at their heels. "Tell me all about it, Signor – um?"

"Renzo, Renzo Agerosi – the

unhappy Renzo, who has lost one of the greatest treasures ever found in this greatest of cities!"

McCann flung himself into a chair and pressed his fingertips together, a gesture Bob knew of old, a gesture that meant McCann's razor-sharp brain was paying microscopic attention. "Tell me," he demanded.

Renzo unfolded his sad tale. The lion is the great symbol of Venice, he explained. One of the Venetian cleaning barges had discovered, quite by chance, beneath the dark waters of a canal, a solid gold lion weighing 20 pounds, covered in the slime of centuries.

Renzo, a great Italian art expert, had arranged for art specialists from all over the world to see the marvellous thing, and to discuss the work at leisure. They had arrived the previous night, all of them staying in a magnificent palace, a palazzo on the Grand Canal itself. Each had been given his own room opening onto the Grand Hall.

That morning, before any of the experts in the palazzo was stirring, Renzo arrived, carrying the great golden lion, ready to give his guests their first sight of the treasure. He placed it reverently on a plinth in the centre of the hall, but a telephone call in his office in the palazzo had summoned him, and he left the lion unguarded for two minutes while he courteously listened to the apologies for absence from some art expert he had never heard of.

When he returned, the lion was gone.

"It is a tragedy," he moaned. "To think that only this morning I discovered that the book – the lion of Venice, he always holds a book – but this golden book actually opens and closes! It is a unique work because of this and no one knows except for me. And now maybe the thief, he will melt my statue! Oh, I am desolated!"

"I think there's little I can do from here," remarked McCann drily. "Signor Agerosi, take me to your palazzo."

The trio rushed to catch one of the many boats that serve as buses in Venice. No gondola for them: they were in a hurry.

In the Grand Hall of the palazzo, the situation was chaotic. Fourteen of the world's top art experts were milling around the plinth where the lion had stood for so few moments. Swiftly, McCann introduced himself and found time to exchange a few words with each of them.

There was a very correct Englishman called Hargreaves: "It's a frightful blow," he said, "though I must say, I'm a paintings man myself. Carpaccio's my thing, as they say – and he never had anything to do with metal, of course."

"I'm a specialist in ze metal," said Schulter Reimhug a crusty whiskered Austrian. "I am particularly interested in how zis liddle thing did not rust after so many years under water."

A sinister looking expert from Russia, known only as Illyushin, said grimly: "I think the lion is very symbolic of both war and peace."

But a fat and breezy American from the University of East Virginia, Homer B. Renryski ignored him: "I am just so upset about this gorgeous, gorgeous lion. The photographs were so great, and I loved the cute way the little book opens and closes."

McCann cleared his throat. "Just wait here a moment will you. Bob and I must look at your rooms. I'm sure you understand the necessity."

"Ah, nyet, nyet," the Russian began to complain, but was stopped by the stout, friendly Renryski: "I guess we just gotta to do as these guys say, Illyushin, baby."

"That's right," said McCann, and he and Bob went through each of the fourteen rooms with brisk efficiency. All were much the same. None hid the lion. Each had a bedside phone, a big four-poster bed, and a key on the inside in each keyhole. Renryski's key seemed to have fallen on the floor. McCann picked it up and replaced it. "Hmm," he said.

McCann and Bob rejoined the group. Bob instantly turned his attention to the faces. From the Russian's grim visage he could read nothing. But Renryski looked ready to cry.

"Oh, Lord, and I was hoping, so much hoping you would find the lion," he said sadly. "That's too bad, I'm real cut up."

"I expect you are," said McCann smoothly. "A lovely piece of Venetian art, by all accounts."

"Oh yes, and I just *love* everything about Venice, I'm a real specialist in everything to do with Venice, that's why I got myself invited here. I've been to Venice just hundreds of times, it's my second home, kind of."

"What do you think of the lion from the photographs?" McCann quizzed.

"Well, it's kinda difficult to tell from a picture, but I'll confess to you that I have a teeny weeny hunch that it's Carpaccio. It looks like a real typical piece of Carpaccio goldwork to me."

"Why do you like Venice so much?" put in Bob.

"They're great people – can you think of anyone else on earth who would flood the streets of their city to keep their enemies out? Sensational! But look, Mr McCann, if it's OK with you, I must, like, scram. I have to meet some guys downtown. I'm late already and I have to catch me a gondola."

"Not so fast, Mr Renryski," rasped McCann. "I'd be happy if you didn't catch this gondola – or any other, for that matter."

"What is all this?" demanded Renryski turning white. The Russian stared at his sudden change.

McCann looked as grim as a lion of war: "OK, hold it right there. We know you saw Renzo here carry the lion into the Grand Hall. We know you had an accomplice who faked the phone call that distracted Renzo for two precious minutes. And what's more, we know you pinched the lion!" Suddenly there was steel in McCann's voice. "Where is it, Renryski?"

Renryski collapsed into a chair, tears starting from his eyes at this horror. "You are the devil himself," he sobbed. "You knew all along. Yes, I stole it. I hid it in the pasta bin in the kitchen. I wanted to leave now so I could rescue it before the chef started preparing lunch. You have ruined me! But tell me – I have to know. How did you discover me?"

"Yes," echoed the astounded Renzo. "How did you work this miracle?"

McCann smiled at last. "He made five careless mistakes."

"Fantastico!" exulted Renzo. "Now all we have to do is discover the man's accomplice – but that won't be easy, I think."

"I don't know about that," mused McCann. "Bob, have you any ideas?"

Bob started at being called on, and then grinned at his uncle. He turned to face the rank of art experts before him.

Hargreaves shuffled his feet and coughed.

Reimhug, the Austrian, lit a thin cigar with careless ease.

Illyushin, the Russian, met Bob's eye with stony certainty.

Bob didn't hesitate. He walked into the knot of experts and clapped his hand on the shoulder of one of them.

"This is your man," he said.

Reimhug crumpled onto the carpet in a dead faint, guilt written large on his face.

As Renzo loosed the hapless Austrian's collar, McCann said: "How did you find him out, Bob?"

"Simple," he said. "He made one mistake – just one, but it was very foolish indeed."

"That makes six slip-ups from this pair," said McCann. "It doesn't pay to make mistakes where the Lion of Venice is concerned. They thought they had a lion – but they had caught a tiger by the tail."

"And it turned around and bit," said Bob.

Did you spot the six mistakes?

Check your answers on page 76.

HANGING ON AIR

For centuries, men looked up into the sky and envied the birds. "If they can do it, why can't we?" they wondered as they watched the sea-gulls effortlessly riding on the air, obviously and infuriatingly enjoying themselves. Then 2832 years ago, in 852 B.C. to be precise, King Bladud of Ancient Britain made the challenge. He fitted himself with a pair of wings, climbed up a tall tower, and jumped . . . I regret to say, to his death.

It took another 2635 years for man to get off the ground – and that was in an air balloon. The first winged flight had to wait for Orville Wright which was only 77 years ago!

But it wasn't until 20 years ago that men seriously returned to King Bladud's basic problem. Never mind about power – there is a bird in the air, and here I am on the ground. If I had wings, I could fly like him. And so, 2812 years after King Bladud the first aviation fatality – Hang Gliding was born.

The sport of Hang Gliding has itself claimed a fair number of deaths – so when I decided to investigate it for Blue Peter, I decided, in the long tradition of the programme, to put myself in the hands of the experts. Gerry Breen has been hang gliding since 1973. He's actually made it – with the help of a small engine and a pair of canvas wings – across the English Channel. He showed me on the day we met that with the same small engine he could perform aerobatics with as much ease as the pilot of a light aircraft.

But I was more interested in the original challenge. No motor – just me – a pair of wings – and the silent, empty air.

We started to unroll the long, thin caterpillar . . .

. . . which emerged as an enormous canvas butterf

High in the hills of Merthyr Tydfil, we found the perfect conditions – clear sky and a 20 mph wind. I helped Gerry unroll the long, thin caterpillar that contained the wings of what was going to become an enormous painted buttefly. Carefully, we fitted battens onto the canvas wings, tightened the nuts, and secured them with pins. Then I put my legs into two mesh stockings which suspended me to the wings.

Because it was my first flight, Gerry had stationed a man on either side of me with a rope tethered to each wing – to keep the glider level.

"They'll hold on to the glider and keep it stable. All you've got to do is to keep those legs down and make a really hard run. You've nothing to worry about – it's only going up to 20 metres." (About two double-decker buses, or four floors of a building, I thought!) "O.K. You're nicely balanced – now, run! Run hard – look at the ground. Pull in – push out – excellent!" I felt the tug of the glider against my thighs as it began to feel the wind – and suddenly, my legs were no longer on the ground. I was airborne! It lasted for about 30 seconds before the ground came up to meet me again.

"Land on the feet," yelled Gerry. My legs were going pell-mell down the hill. I had no hope of keeping my balance and the glider kept pulling me on until I fell headlong into a gorse bush.

"That was fine," said Gerry, as he and the two men heaved me out of the undergrowth. You over controlled it a little – which made you stall – but I don't think you'll make that mistake again." After another couple of goes I began to feel more confident, and more in control of the glider – rather than a dangling creature at the mercy of the wind.

Gerry took me up to the top of the ridge 135 metres above the valley (more than two East Towers, one on top of the other). Next, he removed the rope tethers from each wing.

This time I was on my own.

I began to run – and felt the now familiar tug from the wings as they lifted me into the air. The rush of wind hit my face again, but this time there were no tethers – and I soared into the air. Down below I could see Gerry, a tiny speck as he guided me through the walkie talkie.

"That's great, Chris. A little more to your left – more left – more still. Now straighten up. Push out. Push out."

Down below me a kestrel was riding the thermals as he looked for his prey. Suddenly he dropped like a stone, and then, changing his mind about 60cm. from the ground, he wheeled round and soared effortlessly back to his vantage point. "We've come on a bit since King Bladud," I thought, "but you birds have still got the edge!"

JAPANESE KOI

Goldie and Jack and Jill may be examples of Britain's most popular pets, but in Japan it's not cats and dogs that are top of the animals pops – it's Koi!

"It's what?" you may well be saying, just as I did in the Blue Peter office.

"Koi," they said. "Fish – large, beautiful, multicoloured carp. We want you to take Blue Peter cameras and film some."

My eyes lit up – I've always wanted to visit Japan. "When do we fly?" I asked.

"Fly?" said John Adcock, who organises all the Blue Peter filming. "It's only 15 minutes by car from Television Centre!"

My dreams of an expedition to Japan were quickly shattered when John explained that the Koi *he* had in mind were in a back garden in Ickenham. While most people are content with goldfish, businessman Paul Cook keeps his Koi in *his* pond, and he's famous for having one of the best collections in Europe. Even Japanese experts ask him for advice. And that's a huge compliment,

because Koi are so popular in Japan they hold nationwide Koi shows – just like our dog shows. And they even have a Supreme Champion's prize, like Cruft's, where the winning Koi is awarded thousands of pounds.

Paul Cook's back garden pool was *not*, I discovered, like the one in our Italian Sunken Garden. For one thing, it was about ten times bigger – Koi can grow to 1.25 metres in length – and it was heated too.
I arrived at feeding time and discovered it was quite different from sprinkling handfuls of pond pellets over the water. Between them, Paul's 50 Koi got through two gallons of mussels, two pounds of prawns and half a loaf of brown bread!

By now I was fascinated by these unusual fish. Although they were large, they were extremely friendly. "Put your hand in," said Paul. So rather gingerly I did, and lo and behold, one of the biggest of the Koi swam up and nuzzled my fingers as I stroked its back!

"They're very powerful fish," said Paul, "but they never fight and when I introduce newcomers into the pond, they give them extremely friendly greetings."

As dusk fell, we sat on the terrace and watched the flood-lit pool. I may have missed my 9600 mile trip to Tokyo, but with the bright colours of the Koi flashing past, and gentle, oriental music in the background, I felt Japan had well and truly come to Ickenham!

Japanese Cherry Trees

There's a corner of Japan here at Television Centre, too!

It all began with a phone call from the man who's in charge of looking after all the buildings and grounds, David Proudfoot.

"When you next see Percy Thrower," David said, "can you ask him how to plant cherry trees?"

"Plant *what?*" we said.

"Japanese Flowering Cherry Trees – there are 500 of them arriving next week, and I need a bit of expert advice."

David sounded quite worried, and with good reason. It turned out the trees were a present from the President of Nippon TV, Japan's most important Television channel, to the BBC. They'd been given as a goodwill gift after a visit to Japan by the BBC's Managing Director, Alasdair Milne, so it was vital that they were planted properly.

The President of Nippon TV unveiled the commemorative Cherry Tree plaque and we helped Percy show the distinguished guests our Italian Sunken Garden.

A week later the cherry trees arrived – or rather what looked like 500 long, brown sticks.
"That's right," said Percy. "Prunus Serrulata – Japanese Cherry Trees in English. They look as though they've survived the journey perfectly well." You could have fooled us! It was hard to believe the "sticks" would grow leaves, let alone beautiful, pink blossom!

We inspected every patch of earth at Television Centre with Percy, and in the end, he reckoned there was room to plant 8 of the trees in our Blue Peter garden, and 5 along the road from the Main Gate to the East Tower where our office is.

"They need to be at least 9–15 feet apart," Percy explained. "Flowering Cherries grow quite massive roots and branches." That meant there were enough trees for all the BBC's Regional Centres, as well as London. And if they're all as flourishing as the ones we planted with Percy, there should be

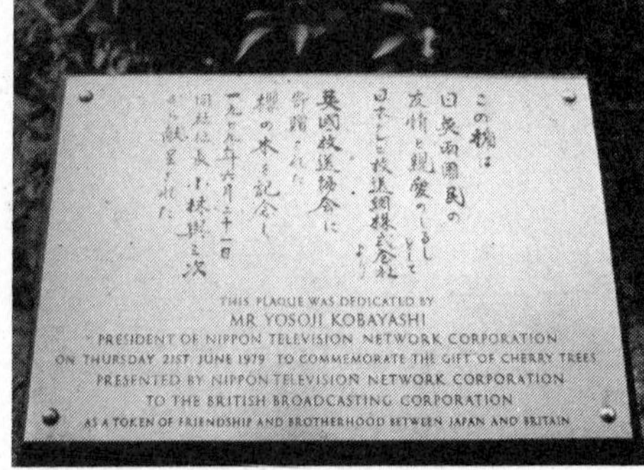

Flowering Cherries in bloom from Inverness to Plymouth next spring. Because Percy was right – the dead-looking sticks *were* alive and well.

Last summer, an impressive ceremony took place – in the pouring rain, just like the day on which we planted the trees! Alasdair Milne, the Heads of BBC 1 and 2, the Head of Children's Programmes and other Top Officials gathered in the garden with us and Percy to welcome the Japanese Ambassador and Mr Yosoji Kobayashi, President of Nippon TV.
A plaque inscribed in both Japanese and English was unveiled to commemorate the gift.

We may not have enough room for Koi in our pond, but we'll always remember Japan when our Flowering Cherries bloom each spring.

It was pitch dark when I first met 14-year-old Jackie Willmott. Every morning she leaves her home at half past four to travel to Southend's Warren Square swimming pool. After that it's on to school for a full day of Maths, English, History and Biology – a tough schedule for one of Britain's top hopes for an Olympic gold medal in the 1980's.

SWIMMING FOR GOLD

If you want to be a world-class swimmer, getting up when most of us are asleep becomes a way of life. Jackie has to travel 5 miles to her pool, and it's only by getting up so early that she can fit in the first couple of hours of her five-hours-a-day training.

Jackie celebrated the start of 1980 by breaking the British Women's 800-metre freestyle record, and she already holds the 1500-metre record. To achieve this kind of result, Jackie swims a gruelling 400 lengths of the Southend pool every day.

I enjoy swimming! At school I took part in lots of competitions, so I looked forward to training with Jackie. But I soon found out just how hard it is, trying to keep up with a world-class swimmer. After half an hour, I was exhausted!

A 1500-metre race is 30 lengths of an Olympic-size pool. During her training, other people swim by her side to help Jackie keep up a regular pace. But like me, after a few lengths, they're whacked, so Jackie always ends up on her own!

8.30

15.05

15.35

As soon as the morning session was over, Jackie grabbed a quick breakfast and made a dash for school. Her headmaster does all he can to help Jackie work for her seven 'O' levels *and* fit in her swimming. She has a special place in the school library and she's allowed to do her homework *before* she leaves school. Jackie's also let out of class ten minutes before everyone else, so that she can catch an early bus – you've guessed it – back to the swimming pool and more training!

During the afternoon training session, Southend pool is open to the public, but one lane is specially roped off for Jackie. By half past five she's covered 10,000 metres – over six miles – wearing a T-shirt this time to weigh her down in the water and make her put even more effort into her strokes. And if she shows signs of flagging, her coach, Mick Higgs, is there to urge her on.

17.30

18.15

Jackie has a good sense of humour. Towards the end of the session she asked me to join her for "one of Mick's special treats" as she put it! This involved swimming flat out for a length, 15 press-ups on the pool side, another length, followed by more press-ups. That's where I gave up – but Jackie continued for another quarter of an hour and didn't even look tired when she'd finished!

By 7 o'clock, we were back at the Willmott's house where Jackie must be one of the few 14-year-olds who has to be in bed by eight o'clock. There was one hour of Jackie's day left for supper and – wait for it – a spot of weight-lifting! But for a special treat, the telly was left on in the background.

In another eight hours Jackie would be back in the pool. If it was left to me – I'd give Jackie a medal now!

19.00

"I wish I could draw!"

Before the camera was invented, a magazine called *The Illustrated London News* employed artists to draw their news stories. Pageants, disasters at sea, scenes in parliament, were all sketched just as they'd happened in real life. This is exactly what **Bob Broomfield** does for us, on Blue Peter. We use him like a photographer to record the facts about stories that happened long ago – like Grimaldi the Clown, the discovery of the potato, Princess Pocahontas or the Gardening Tradescant family.
To be able to draw realistic pictures you need to know about perspective – to be able to make your flat lines on a flat piece of paper look solid and three – dimensional.

Here are some tips from Bob that should stand you in good stead, even if you never become a great artist!

Perspective as an aid to drawing helps to create the illusion of space, depth and solidity on a flat surface. It is the basis for all realistic drawing. However, it doesn't have to be used in a rigid, mechanical way, but rather as a guideline. Do remember, there is no substitute for your own observation and judgement. If a drawing looks right to you, that's all that matters.

DIMINUTION

One effect of perspective that we're all aware of is that things appear smaller when further away. Why is this? Perhaps the picture above will help to explain. The two trees are the same height. The round tree is further away from the artist than the thin tree. The images of the two trees come together at the eye of the artist. You can see that the thin tree's image must be bigger than the round tree's image from where the artist is sitting.

EYE-LEVEL When you begin a drawing, try to decide where your eye-level is to be. First lightly rule a horizontal pencil-line across the picture at the level you choose. What lies above the line is seen from below, and everything under the line is viewed from above. The HORIZON is another word for eye-level.

To show you just how much your eye-level changes the way things appear, Indigo, Olive and Rose are drawing Muffin, the cat. Each one of them has a different eye-level. On the right are the three views of Muffin that they have.

Indigo's eye-level is quite high and gives him almost a bird's-eye-view of Muffin.

Olive's eye-level is the normal one. This is the most natural viewpoint of the three.

Rose's eye-level is the lowest. It gives her a worm's-eye-view of Muffin.

VANISHING POINTS

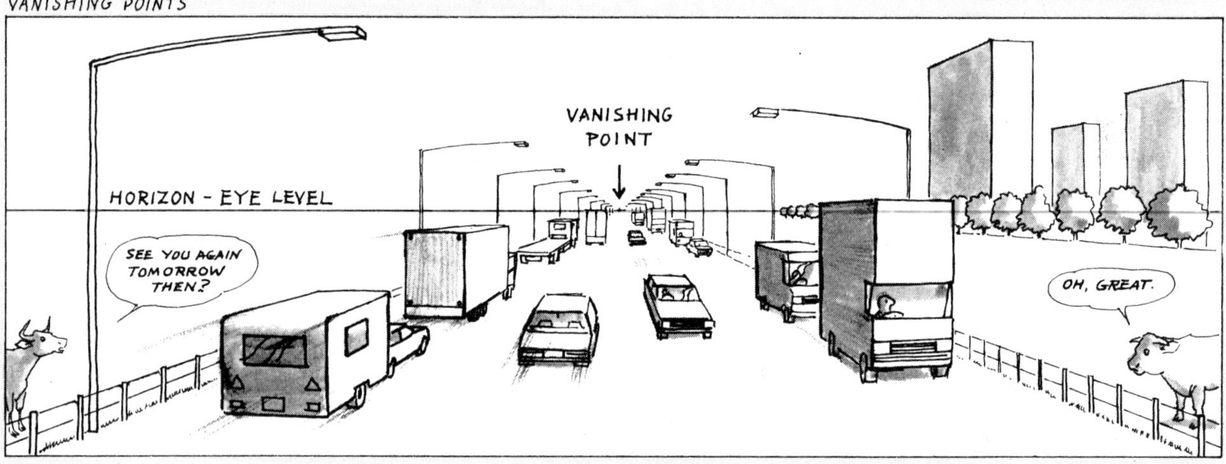

In this sketch, all the lines that are parallel to each other and stretch away into the distance seem to get closer together until they appear to meet at a point on the horizon-eye-level. This is called a VANISHING POINT.

Vanishing points or VPs help us to find the correct angles for the sides of rectangular objects such as buildings or table-tops when drawn in perspective. The picture above has a single VP, but there can be several in one picture.

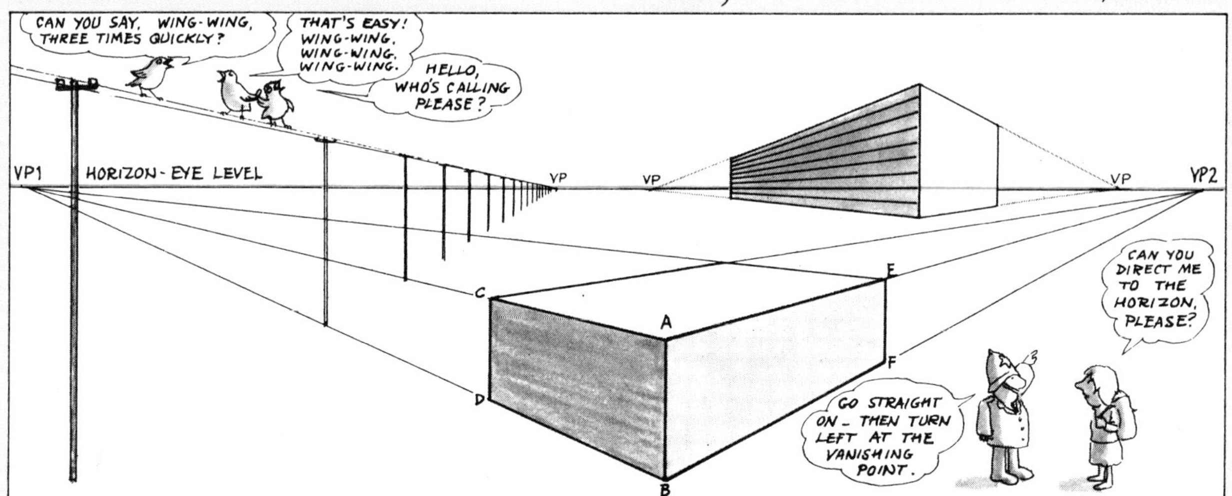

Here are some objects which show the usefulness of vanishing points. Practise by drawing the rectangular block in the centre of the picture. The VPs should be as far apart as the paper size will allow. If they are too close together, the perspective will be very distorted and exaggerated.

First draw the nearest upright AB. Then draw lines from A & B to VP1 on the eye-level. Again, from points A & B draw lines to VP2. Draw in the other uprights, CD & EF. Join C to VP2 and E to VP1 and the rectangle will be complete. Ink in the outline, erase the pencil guidelines, add doors, windows and shadows.

EQUAL DISTANCES IN PERSPECTIVE

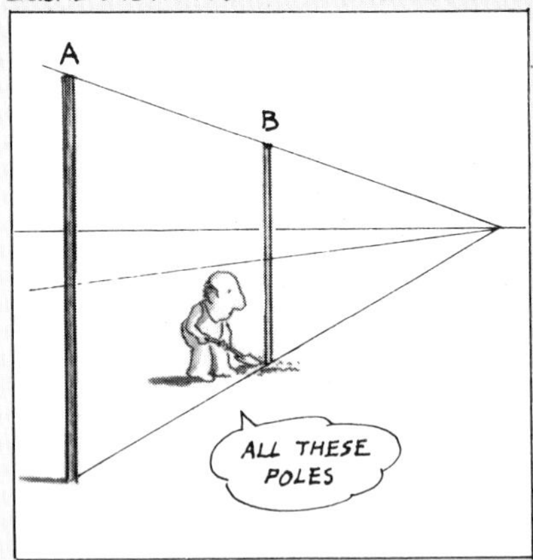

To draw equally spaced poles. Draw first pole A. Lightly pencil in lines from top, centre and bottom of A to a vanishing point on the eye-level line. The centre line will mark the mid-point of all the poles. Draw the next pole B.

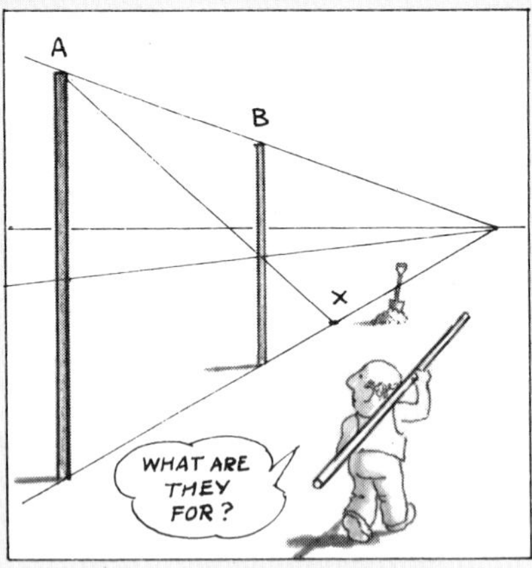

Now draw a diagonal from the top of A through the mid-point of B to the point X on the lower line. X marks the spot where the third pole will be.

Repeat this process for as long as necessary. This method can be used for any evenly-spaced objects.

CIRCLES AND WHEELS IN PERSPECTIVE

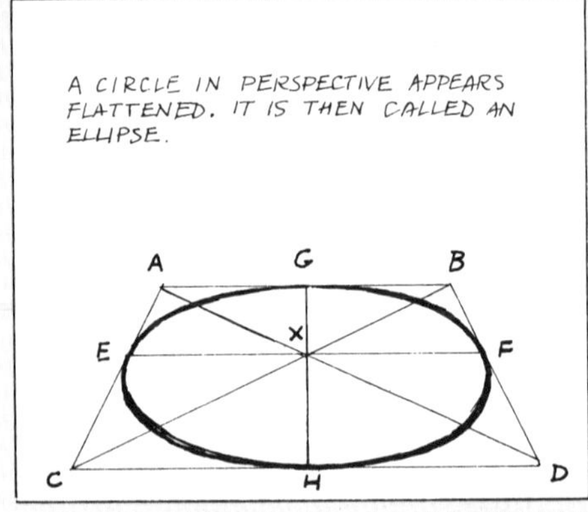

To draw an ellipse, enclose it in a square ABCD, which is drawn in perspective. Draw diagonals AD and BC. Where these diagonals cross at X, draw lines EF and GH. Carefully draw in the ellipse so it touches points EFGH.

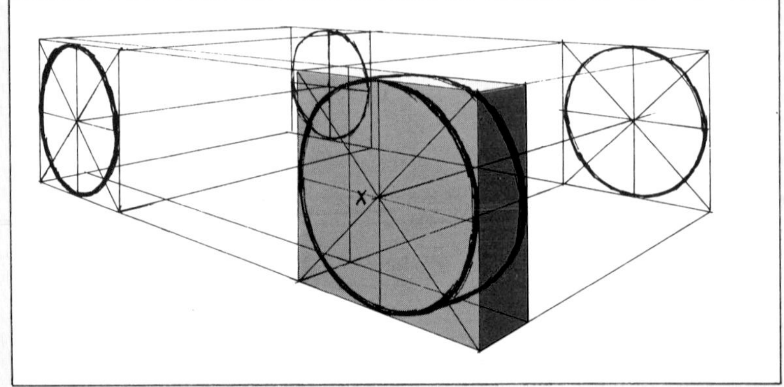

When a wheel is in perspective, we see it as a vertical ellipse. Draw a box in perspective as if enclosing the wheel, then draw in the ellipses as before. The wheel axle always passes through the point where the two diagonals of the square cross as at X.

SHADOWS

The type of light affects the way a shadow is cast. We regard the sun's rays to be parallel. Artificial light radiates from a point at the centre of the source. The object and its cast shadow will have the same vanishing points.

ARTIFICIAL LIGHT

Draw lines from the lamp through the top corners of the box, AB&C. From the point, P, directly under the lamp, draw lines through the bottom corners, EF&G. Join up where the lines meet at XY&Z.

SUNLIGHT

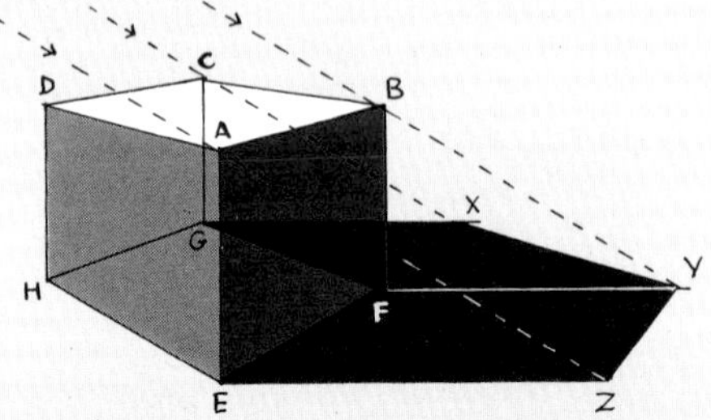

To find the shadow of the box when the sun is on one side. Draw parallel lines on the ground from the box. Then draw more parallel lines from the sun, through corners AB&C to meet lines through EF&G at points XY&Z. This forms the shadow area.

REFLECTIONS

The reflection of an object in still water has the same measurements as the object. The same vanishing points are used for both the object and image. But the reflection will appear as if seen from a lower eye-level, so a slightly different aspect of the reflected object is seen. It's best to draw the complete reflection first, then erase where the image is interrupted.

Reflections on rippling water become distorted and broken up. If the water's surface is more disturbed the reflection will appear longer.

AERIAL PERSPECTIVE

The more distant an object is, the less distinct it becomes. Details disappear, colours begin to soften, dark and light tones become greyer until they merge into one tone. Think of hills far away in the distance, they can appear as a uniform bluish-grey, although you know they are green and colourful and perhaps dotted with trees and bushes. This is called aerial perspective or sometimes, atmospheric perspective, because it's the atmosphere between us and the distant view that blurs the details. This is very useful for outdoor scenes when you may want to show that one object lies behind or further away than another.

Finally, here are two pictures of the same scene. The one below has seven errors of perspective. Can you find them?

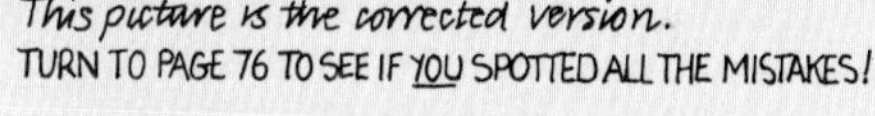

This picture is the corrected version.
TURN TO PAGE 76 TO SEE IF YOU SPOTTED ALL THE MISTAKES!

FLOWER POWER

Nearly 40,000 viewers entered our Flower Picture Competition. The idea was to paint or draw a sketch for a picture to be made completely out of flowers for display at Westminster Cathedral's Festival of Flowers. And your ideas helped to provide £30,000 for the International Year of the Child, because the proceeds of the festival were donated to that very good cause.

We asked you to sketch something you thought would make children of *all* nationalities happy, so it was an extremely cheerful competition to judge. There were favourite toys, pets, mouth-watering foods like ice creams and jellies, exciting holiday scenes and clowns and Father Christmases and panto characters by the score.

For our nine Top Prize Winning Sketches, we chose a clown, a dove of peace, a butterfly and an owl, a parrot and a bumble bee, a teddy and a white rabbit. And the Overall Top Prize Winning Sketch was a cuddly koala bear sent in by Sarah Holloway of Leicester.

All these were transformed into Flower Pictures by expert flower arranger Margaret Ferguson, with the help of Elizabeth Baker, Alix Hare and Rose Minter and displayed in the Chancel of the Cathedral. And on Friday, 13 July, the nine Blue Peter prize winners came to London for the most memorable day of their lives.

The reason? None other than to be presented to Her Majesty the Queen!

Eight of the nine Top Prize Winners in the Blue Peter studio with their award winning sketches. Lesley Fish had arrived late due to an 'O' level exam!

120 Runners-Up sketches were displayed in the Cathedral gallery.

It was to be a truly historic day, for it was the first-ever visit of a reigning monarch to the Cathedral – the Cathedral church of Cardinal Hume who is head of the Roman Catholic Church in England and Wales.

Our flower pictures were only part of the Festival. The whole Cathedral was to be decorated, and two days beforehand, it was a hive of activity. There were to be displays in each of the nine Cathedral Chapels as well as the Baptistery, the Sanctuary and the High Altar, the Porch, the Alcoves and the pillars. It was a colossal race against the clock to get them

ready. Thousands of flowers had to be arranged, and buckets of them spread as far as the eye could see. The nave was being transformed into an avenue of 32 flowering trees, each one bearing 290 white blooms. The air was filled with the most delicious mixture of scents, and when the public was admitted on Thursday, 12 July, you could watch people's faces wreathed in

A final word with the Winners before the Queen and the Duke of Edinburgh arrived.

smiles as they both saw and *smelt* the displays.

On Friday the 13th, huge crowds lined up for the climax of the Festival many hours before the Queen was due to arrive.

Inside, we'd been preparing for the moment when Her Majesty reached the Chancel and the Blue Peter display.

Each winner stood next to his or her picture and practised bows and curtsies – or rather, nods and bobs. I was going to present each person, after the Duchess of Norfolk, who'd organised the festival, had presented me to the Queen. It was really quite simple. I had to go down the line and say "Ma'am", remembering to make it rhyme with "ham" and not with "arm", "may I present Sarah Holloway," – or whichever winner we'd reached. Then the boys would bow – not a deep bow from the waist, just a nod, and the girls would curtsy with a small bend of the knees, not swooping right down to the ground.

What I *didn't* know was how long

The Arundel Carpet was the centrepiece of the Festival. It took five arrangers seven hours to complete.

the Queen would want to stay with each person. Time was really very short – her schedule for touring the whole Cathedral, including more than 50 flower arrangements plus a special presentation, only amounted to 45 minutes, it was all rather nerve-racking, and I must confess, my mouth went dry when I heard the cheers of the crowds outside, which meant that the Royal Party had arrived.

There was a positive barrage of flashes from the press cameras as they and the film and TV cameramen recorded the moment the Queen, followed by the Duke of Edinburgh, set foot inside the Cathedral. Then the choristers sang the National Anthem more beautifully than I'd ever heard it before – the Royal visit had well and truly begun.

In the end, it all happened so quickly my nervousness vanished. The Queen, dressed in a floaty dress and matching coat of soft, pale green chiffon, with a matching broad-brimmed hat encircled with flowers, put us all at our ease. She was extremely interested in the pictures, especially the parrot designed by Rebecca Howse which Her Majesty thought looked more like a toucan, and she seemed amused when, on the spur of the moment, I said Jenny Lingham's clown, with his large, spotted bow tie, looked like a happy Robin Day.

But there was no doubt that Sarah's Koala was the highlight of the display. I explained that by winning the competition, Sarah was to have the holiday of a lifetime, as a guest of a Spanish organisation called Operación Plus Ultra Internacionale, and that she would visit Mexico and the United States, meeting the President of Mexico and the Secretary General of the United Nations, Dr Kurt Waldheim. You could tell the Queen was impressed.

The Duchess of Norfolk told the Queen that upstairs, in the Cathedral gallery, the sketches of a hundred and twenty of the competition Runners-Up were being displayed, and then the Royal Party walked over to the centrepiece of the Festival – a 10-metre-long carpet of flowers that had taken five arrangers seven hours to complete, and stretched right up to the Nave. It's called the Arundel Carpet, because every year since 1873, on the Feast of Corpus Christi, it's laid along the aisle of the Cathedral at Arundel.

After that the Queen left. It was almost half past one, and five hours since we'd started our rehearsals. Very kindly, the Cathedral staff had said we could borrow the Choir School library to give the winners and their parents a much needed buffet lunch, so we slipped along the passage by the side of the High Altar that connects the Cathedral to the School, to relax and compare notes.

Even though it had been a long and tiring morning, everyone was bubbling over with excitement. "What did the Queen say?" "Did she like your picture?" "What did you say to her?" Proud Mums and Dads and Grans and Grandads flocked around the winners, anxious to hear every detail of the Queen's reactions. Quietly, the door opened and a very familiar figure indeed walked in. Although Cardinal Hume was due to lunch with a group of bishops, he'd come out of his way to the library especially to meet the prize-winners. Shortly afterwards, two more distinguished visitors arrived – none other than the Duke and Duchess of Norfolk.

"What with the Queen, the Cardinal *and* two Dukes and a Duchess, I'll remember today for ever!" sighed one of the winners. I think we'd all agree it was certainly our lucky Friday the Thirteenth!

The Queen shook hands with all the winners as I introduced them to her.

Cardinal Hume and the Duchess of Norfolk joined all of us at lunch after the Queen left.

Now find a mirror!

SOLUTIONS

Puzzle Pictures

1 Goldie makes friends with **top Russian gymnasts, Nelli Kim, Bogdan Makuts and Natalia Shaposhnikova.**

2 Animal expert, **George Cansdale, celebrated his 70th birthday** on Blue Peter by blowing out the candles on his birthday snake cake.

3 Retired schoolteacher, **Elsie Whitehead,** brought **Blue Peter Guide Dog Buttons** to the studio when she told us about the sad death of Honey, the programme's first "eyes for the blind".

4 **Puppeteer, Bert Bowden,** who demonstrated his amazing skills in the studio.

5 **Percy Thrower** admires **"Super Carrot",** grown in **Huddersfield** by **Alfred Howcroft.** It tipped the scales at a colossal 7 lb. 11½ oz. (3.5 kg) and had a 19" (48 cm) waist!

6 **Viscount Montgomery of Alamein** towered above us in the studio. This was the **prototype for a statue** unveiled in his honour by the **Queen Mother** on the grass outside the **Ministry of Defence in Whitehall.**

7 **Toco the Toucan** from Twycross Zoo showing off **his bill repaired with fibre glass.**

8 **Monsieur Dobouljinsky,** creator of the world's most realistic animal masks.

9 **Prize-winning soloists in the National Brass Contest,** Stephen Ruck and Bill Millar. Stephen was the first Blue Peter viewer ever to play a cornet on the programme with a broken arm. Bill was a semi-finalist in the Young Musician of the Year Competition.

10 Making friends with **Champion Police Dog, Samson,** and his handler PC John Fleet.

The Case of the Lion of Venice

1 Renzo told McCann that no one in the world except he knew the lion's book opened and closed – but Renryski knew. He must have seen the lion to know that.

2 The key in Renryski's room was found on the floor. McCann deduced that Renryski had been watching Renzo through the keyhole when he left the lion unguarded.

3 Renryski made the mistake of thinking Carpaccio worked in gold – though McCann had just learnt from the English expert that Carpaccio was a painter, and never worked in metals.

4 Renryski, a self-styled expert on Venice, thought the canals were created by flooding the streets. McCann had already given Bob the true explanation for the city's canals.

5 Renryski said Venice was his second home – but, even though he was in a hurry, he told McCann he was going to catch a gondola. McCann knew that only tourists with plenty of time used gondolas.

6 Reimhug revealed that he could not be a metal specialist when he remarked that the lion might have rusted beneath the water. Gold does not rust.

I wish I could draw!

1 The bird on the tree is too big.

2 The man and the boat are also too big.

3 The reflection of the tree is not under the tree.

4 The man's reflection shouldn't be sloping.

5 The chimney is seen from the wrong eye-level.

6 The shadows of the house and chimney stack are in the wrong direction.

7 The oil drum ellipses shouldn't slope.

Three of the donations to our Great Blue Peter Bring and Buy Sale Auction. A Coldstream Guards NCO's scarlet tunic, a Victorian dress and parasol, and the space suit belonging to Sting of the Police.

ACKNOWLEDGEMENTS

Co-ordinator: **Gillian Farnsworth**

Designed by: **David Playne** assisted by Robert Ayliffe, Laurie Clark and Jon Davis

Christmas Garlands and Football Game by **Margaret Parnell.**

Queen Matilda's Strip Cartoon, Abbey National! and "Here We Are Again!" were written by **Dorothy Smith.**

The pyramid (p. 46/47) and "Here We Are Again!" were illustrated by **Robert Broomfield.**

Photographs in this book were taken by John Adcock, David Clarke, Laurie Clark, Michael Cullen, Conrad Hafenrichter, Robert Hill, Tim Jenkins, Tom Johnson, Peter Lane, Oxfam, David Playne, Joan Williams, Associated Press and R.N.A.S. Culdrose.
with the exception of
Domesday Book (p. 14) from the Public Record Office.
William the Conqueror (p. 14) by BBC Hulton Picture Library.
Westminster Abbey photographs (p. 36–37) by Perfecta Publications Ltd.;
Tutankhamun (p. 49) by Robert Harding Associates.
Cathedral photographs (p. 51) by Durham Cathedral.
The Nave (p. 72) and Arundel Carpet (p. 74) by permission of the Friends of Westminster Cathedral.

USEFUL INFORMATION

Westminster Cathedral
Ashley Place, London S.W.1.
Open: 8.00–8.00p.m.

Bayeux Tapestry
Bayeux, Normandy, France.
There is an excellent replica at the Reading Museum and Art Gallery, where one panel is always on view and there are regular exhibitions of the entire tapestry.

Clowns' Service
Holy Trinity Church, Dalston.

Egyptian Tourist Centre
62a Piccadilly, London W.1.

Durham Knocker
Cathedral Treasury, Durham.
Open: Monday–Saturday, 10.30 – 4.00 p.m. Sunday, 2.00 – 4.00 p.m.
35p adults, 10p children.

Royal Navy Air Station Culdrose
Helston, Cornwall.

Westminister Abbey
London S.W.1.
Open: 8.00 – 6.00 p.m. Entry to Royal Chapels: 80p. adults, 10p. children

British Hang Gliding Association
167a Cheddon Road, Taunton, Somerset TA2 7AH.

Blue Peter Book of Gorgeous Grub
published by Piccolo/BBC, price 75p.

BLUE PETER COMPETITION

Would you like to come to the Television Centre and see the Blue Peter studio? Would you like to meet the Blue Peter team and all the animals?

This could be your chance to come to London and meet them all at a special party if you win our EYE SPY competition.

All these eyes belong to famous personalities who appear regularly on BBC TV Children's programmes. Send us a list numbered 1 – 16 with the names of the stars whose eyes we've photographed. Remember to attach the official entry form to your list – otherwise we won't know who you are!

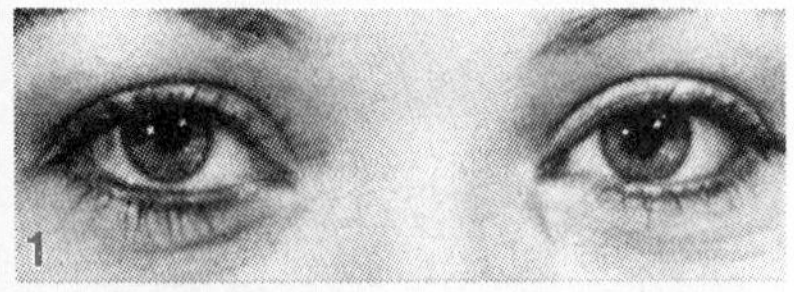
1

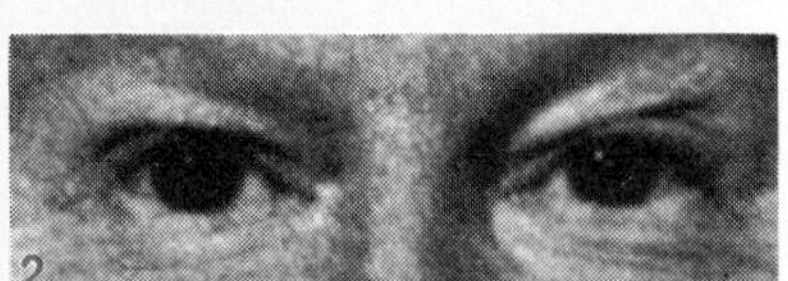
2

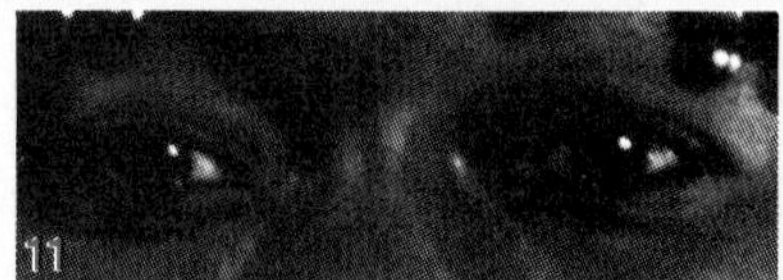
11

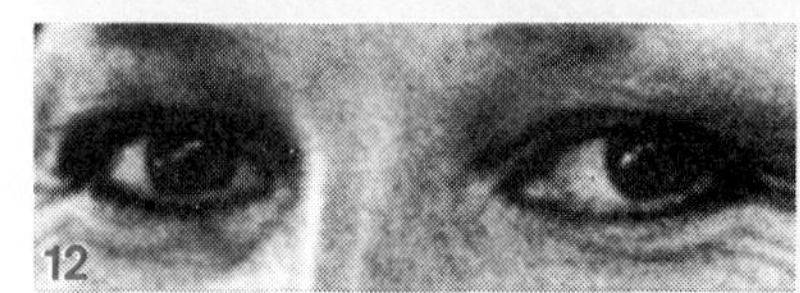
12

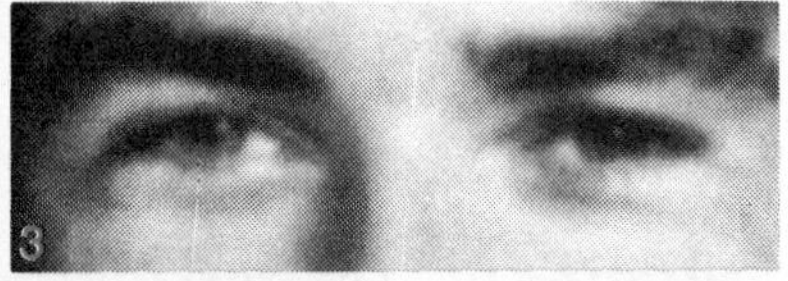
3

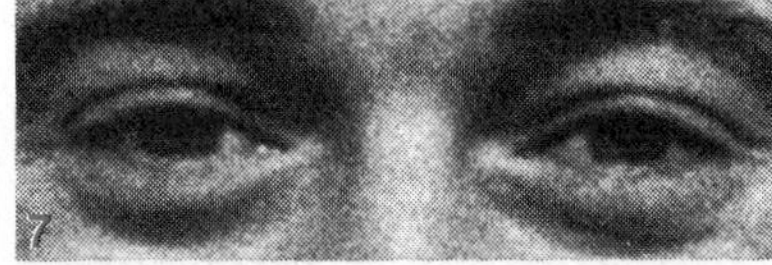
7

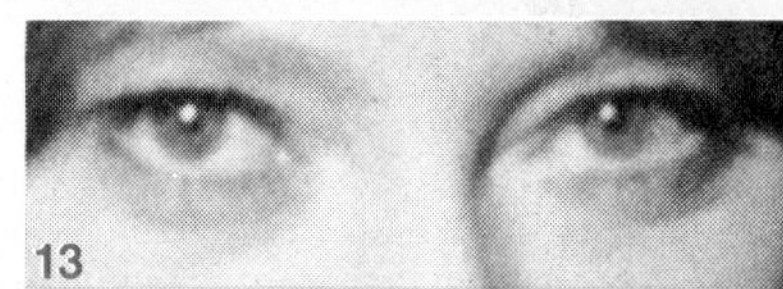
13

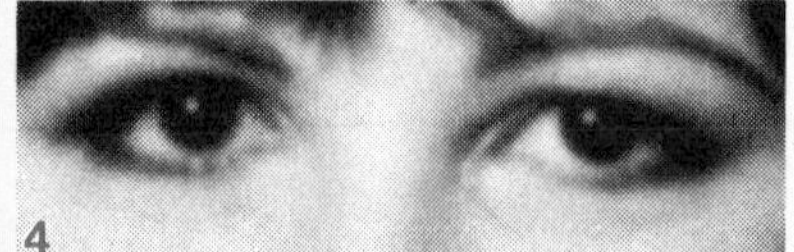
4

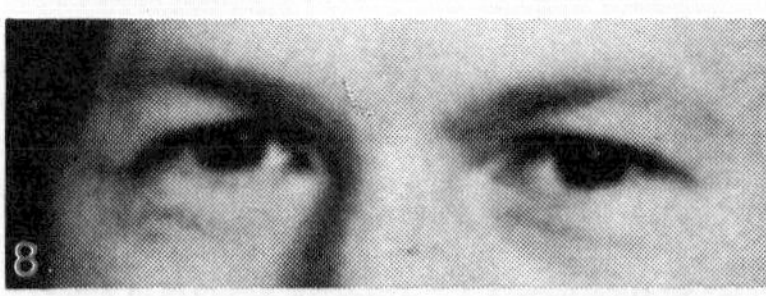
8

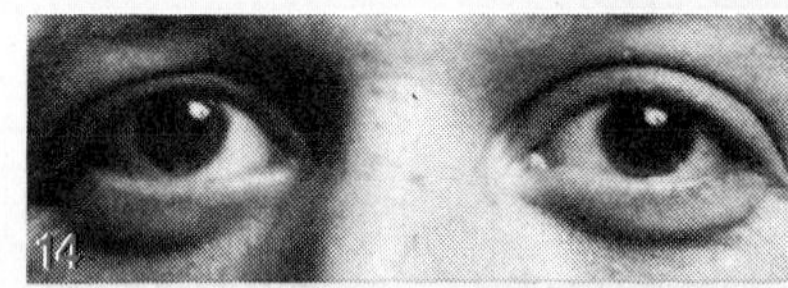
14

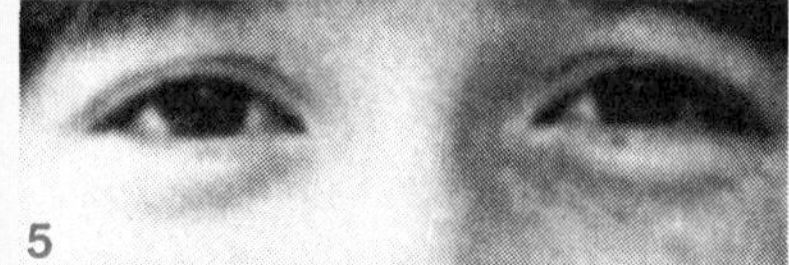
5

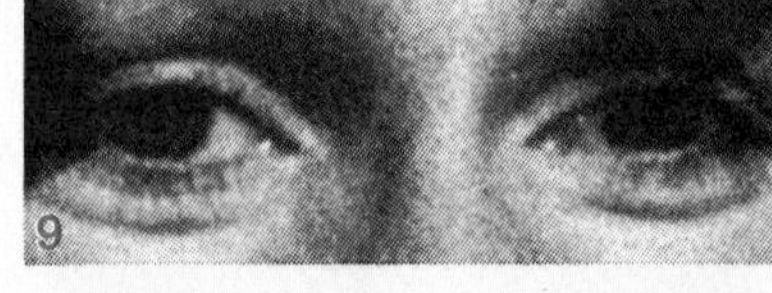
9

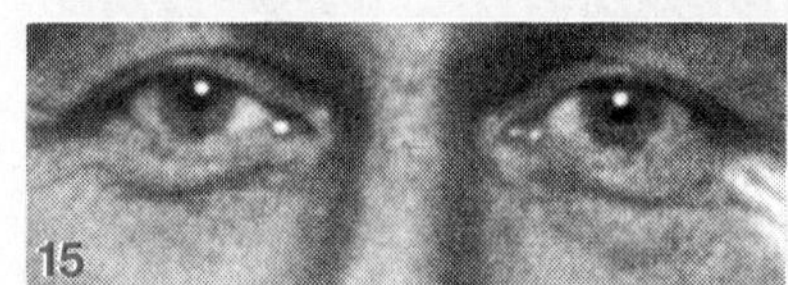
15

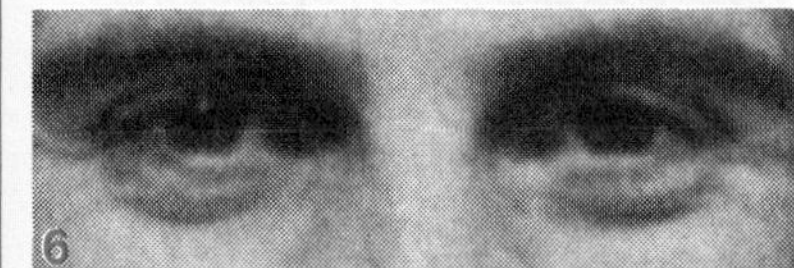
6

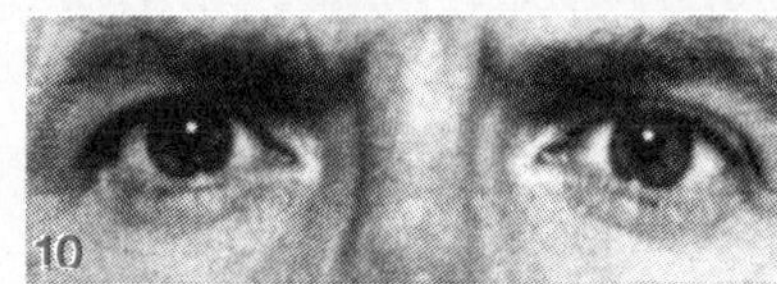
10

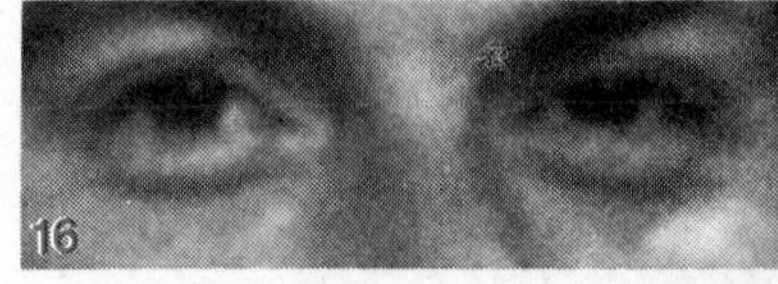
16

First prize winners and runners-up will be notified by letter. **Closing date: 10 January 1981.**

Twenty-four people who send us the correct answers will be invited to our

BLUE PETER PARTY

and there'll be lots of competition badges for the runners-up, too!

Competition Address:
Eye Spy, Blue Peter, BBC TV Centre, London W12 7RJ.

Name: ______________________

Age: __________

Address: ______________________

____

____

1
18
14
19
13
10
9
11
12